Alfred's Essentials of MUSIC THEORY

TEACHER'S

Lessons • Ear Training • Workbook

ANDREW SURMANI • KAREN FARNUM SURMANI • MORTON MANUS

FOREWORD

Listening to music is one of the most popular pastimes, enjoyed by people all over the world. Whether listening to recordings or attending live concerts, music has the ability to inspire and give pleasure to almost everyone.

For many students and professionals, playing a musical instrument is an even more enjoyable experience. But understanding how music is constructed; how scales and chords are formed; the relationship between major and minor keys; and how music is composed through melody, harmony and chord progressions can enhance the musical experience even further. There is also current scientific research which proves that studying music improves I.Q. scores—it actually makes students smarter.

Alfred's Essentials of Music Theory is designed for students of any age, whether listener or performer, who want to have a better understanding of the language of music.

BOOKS 1, 2, 3: This theory course is made up of three books of 40 pages each, with each book containing six units. A unit consists of four or five pages of instructional material (including written exercises), an Ear Training page and a Review page.

Each new term is capitalized the first time it is introduced (GRAND STAFF) and will also be listed in the Glossary & Index of Terms and Symbols (along with the page number) at the end of each book. As the Glossary only contains terms introduced within the book, it is a complete listing of subjects included.

COMPLETE BOOK: *Alfred's Essentials of Music Theory* is also available in one complete book of 120 pages that contains all the pages included in the separate books. An alto clef (viola) edition is also available in one complete or three separate books.

TEACHER'S ANSWER KEY: A *Complete Book* with the answers for the exercises from the Lesson and Review pages and music for the Ear Training pages. Also included is a reproducible sheet for listing student names and grades for the Ear Training and Review pages.

COMPACT DISCS: One of the difficulties in studying music theory is not being able to hear what is being learned. The two CDs available (**CD 1** covers Books 1 and 2, **CD 2** covers Book 3) not only allow the student to hear the musical elements discussed, but offers the student opportunities to test their listening skills. Musical examples are played by a variety of instruments (piano, flute, clarinet, alto saxophone, trumpet, trombone, violin and cello).

COMPUTER SOFTWARE: The use of computers in the music studio has become commonplace in many schools and universities. *Alfred's Essentials of Music Theory* offers companion software for both IBM-compatible and Macintosh computers that will allow the instructor to test and drill students, keep track of their students' progress, and make use of interactive instruction in the classroom.

Thanks to:
John O'Reilly, E.L. Lancaster,
Matt McKagan, Todd Helm
and especially Bruce Goldes.

TABLE OF CONTENTS
Book 1

Table of Contents Book 2
See page 42

Table of Contents Book 3
See page 82

The Staff, Notes and Pitches

Music is written on a STAFF of five lines and the four spaces between.

The STAFF

Music NOTES are oval-shaped symbols that are placed *on* the lines and *in* the spaces. They represent musical sounds, called PITCHES.

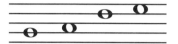

The lines of the staff are numbered from bottom to top.

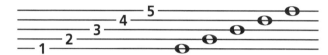

The spaces between the lines are also numbered from bottom to top.

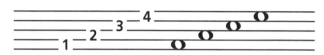

If the notes appear *higher* on the staff, they sound *higher* in pitch.
If the notes appear *lower* on the staff, they sound *lower* in pitch.

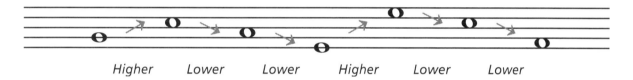

Higher   Lower   Lower   Higher   Lower   Lower

Exercises

* 1 Draw a staff by connecting the dots. Use a ruler or straight edge. Number the lines, then the spaces from low to high.

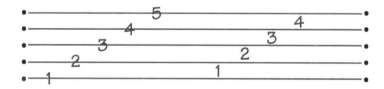

2 On the staff, mark an **X** in the following locations:

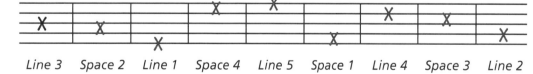

Line 3   Space 2   Line 1   Space 4   Line 5   Space 1   Line 4   Space 3   Line 2

3 Write notes like this ○ on the following lines and spaces:

Space 4   Line 1   Space 2   Line 3   Space 1   Line 5   Space 3   Line 2   Line 4

4 Indicate whether the 2nd note is higher or lower than the 1st note by using an H (higher) or L (lower).

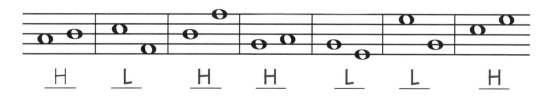

H   L   H   H   L   L   H

*Correct answers are indicated in grey.

Treble Clef and Staff

Music notes are named after the first seven letters of the alphabet, from A to G.
By their position on the staff, they can represent the entire range of musical sound.

CLEF signs help to organize the staff so notes can easily be read.

The TREBLE CLEF is used for notes in the higher pitch ranges. The treble (or G) clef has evolved from a stylized letter G:

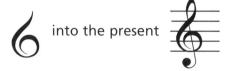 into the present

The curl of the treble clef circles the line on which the note G is placed. This G is above MIDDLE C (the C nearest the middle of the keyboard).

The TREBLE STAFF

 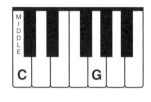

In the treble staff, the names of the notes on the lines from bottom to top are E, G, B, D, F.

Line Notes

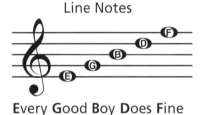

Every **G**ood **B**oy **D**oes **F**ine

The names of the notes in the spaces from bottom to top spell FACE.

Space Notes

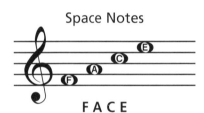

F A C E

All the notes of the TREBLE STAFF:

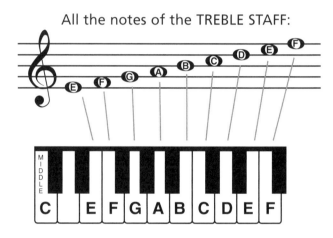

Exercises

1 The treble clef is written in two motions. Trace along the dotted lines as indicated, then draw four more.

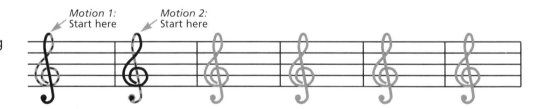

Motion 1: Start here   Motion 2: Start here

2 Write the letter names of the following notes. Use capital letters.

C G F B F E E A D C

3 Write the notes on the staff indicated by the letters. If the notes can be written in two places, write one above the other.

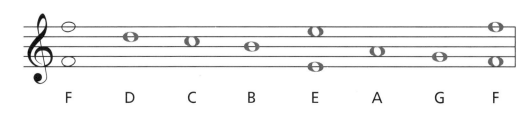

F   D   C   B   E   A   G   F

Bass Clef and Staff

The BASS CLEF (pronounced "base") is used for notes in the lower pitch ranges. The bass (or F) clef has evolved from a stylized letter F:

 into the present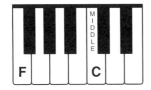

The BASS STAFF

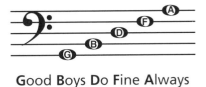

The two dots of the bass clef surround the line on which the note F is placed. This F is below middle C.

Line Notes

All the notes of the BASS STAFF:

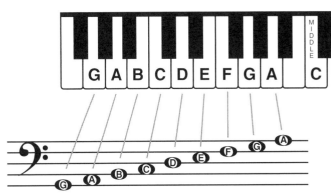

In the bass staff, the names of the notes on the lines from bottom to top are G, B, D, F, A.

Good **B**oys **D**o **F**ine **A**lways

Space Notes

The names of the notes in the spaces from bottom to top are A, C, E, G.

All **C**ows **E**at **G**rass

Exercises

1 The bass clef is written in four motions. Trace along the dotted lines as indicated, then draw four more.

Motion 1: Dot on 4th line   *Motion 2:* Curved line   *Motions 3 & 4:* Dots surrounding 4th line

2 Write the letter names of the following notes.

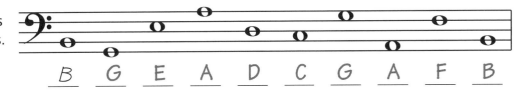

B   G   E   A   D   C   G   A   F   B

3 Write the notes on the staff indicated by the letters. If the notes can be written in two places, write one above the other.

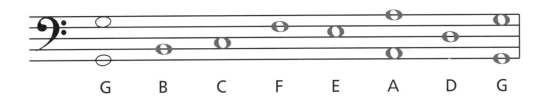

G   B   C   F   E   A   D   G

The Grand Staff

When the bass and treble staffs are connected by a brace and a line, they combine to form the GRAND STAFF.

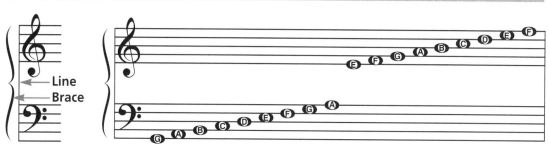

Ledger Lines — The Middle Notes

LEDGER LINES are short lines which are added to extend the range of the staff when the notes are too low or too high to be written on the staff.

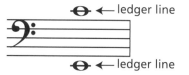

The notes in the middle range of the grand staff are B, C and D.
They can be written on ledger lines in both the bass and treble staffs.

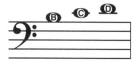 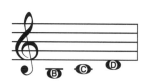 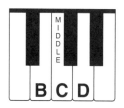 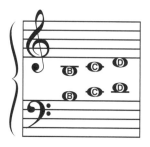

These notes are written differently but sound the same.

Exercises

1 Trace these three braces. Then, using the staffs provided, draw the grand staff three times. Include the brace, line and both clef signs.

2 Write the letter names of the notes from the treble staff.

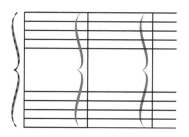

D B B A E C G D E D B C C F F

3 Write the letter names of the notes from the bass staff.

C D B F C D G C B G B A A D E

4 Write the notes indicated by the clefs and letter names in two places on the grand staff. Add ledger lines where necessary.

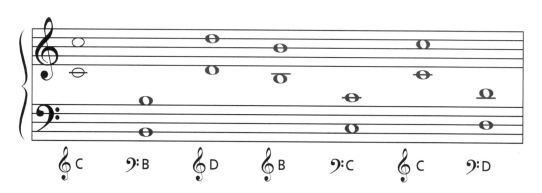

Ledger Lines
Low and High Notes

More than one ledger line may be added to extend the lower and upper ranges of the grand staff. The next higher notes of the treble staff are G, A, B and C.

The next lower notes of the bass staff are F, E, D and C.

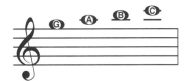

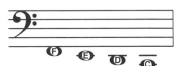

All the notes on the grand staff from bass clef Low C to treble clef High C:

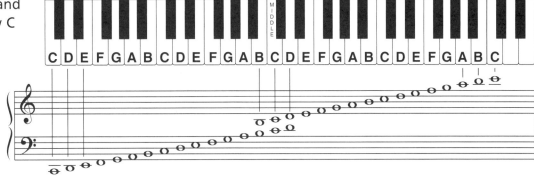

Exercises

1 Draw a treble clef and name the notes.

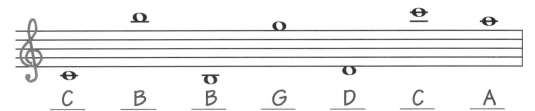

C   B   B   G   D   C   A

2 Draw a bass clef and name the notes.

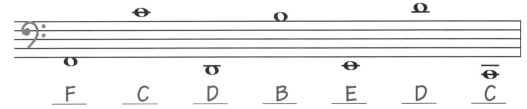

F   C   D   B   E   D   C

3 Write each of the indicated notes in four places on the grand staff.

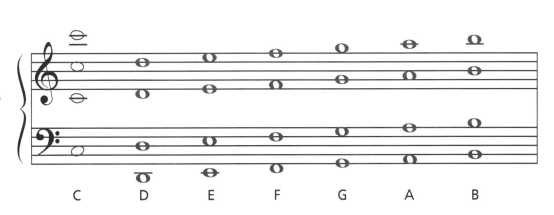

C   D   E   F   G   A   B

Examples:

Page 8 from the Student Book:

a. b.

c.  d.

e.  f.

2

a. 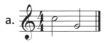 b.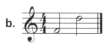

c.  d.

e.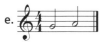

3

a.  b.

c.  d.

e. 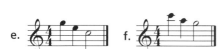 f.

4

8

UNIT 1 **EAR TRAINING FOR LESSONS 1–5**

Low and High

Track 1*
1 You will hear low and high sounds.
Circle low if you hear low sounds; circle high if you hear high sounds.

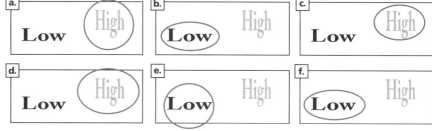

Track 2
2 Listen to the examples and indicate whether the second note is lower (L) or higher (H).

a. __L__   b. __H__   c. __H__   d. __L__   e. __H__

Up and Down

Track 3
3 You will hear three sounds that go up or down. Circle the arrow pointing up if the sounds go up or circle the arrow pointing down if the sounds go down.

Track 4
4 Listen to the notes in the treble clef. The notes will be played from low to high in ascending order.

Track 5
5 Listen to the notes in the bass clef. The notes will be played from low to high in ascending order.

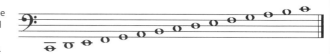

Track 6
6 Listen to the following notes and indicate whether they sound like they should be notated in the bass clef or treble clef (mark with a B or T).

a. __T__ b. __B__ c. __B__ d. __T__ e. __T__ f. __B__ g. __T__ h. __B__

*Track 1 refers to the track number on Ear Training CD 1.

5

6

a. b. c.

d. e. f.

g. h.

1 How many lines are on a single staff? ____5____

2 How many spaces are on a single staff? ____4____

3 Is the 5th line at the bottom or top of the staff?
____Top____

4 Which clef is also known as the G clef? ____Treble____

5 The note names of the five lines in the treble clef from bottom to top are:
____E G B D F____ .

6 The note names of the four spaces in the treble clef from bottom to top are:
____F A C E____ .

7 The line through middle C is called a ____ledger____ line.

8 Which clef is also known as the F clef? ____Bass____ .

9 The note names of the five lines in the bass clef from bottom to top are:
____G B D F A____ .

10 The note names of the four spaces in the bass clef from bottom to top are:
____A C E G____ .

11 Write the letter names of the notes.

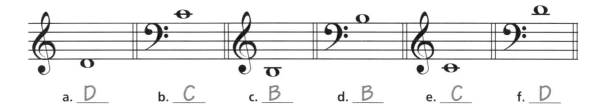

a. D   b. C   c. B   d. B   e. C   f. D

12 Write the letter names of the notes.

G E C F D F A B G C

13 Draw the grand staff and name the notes.

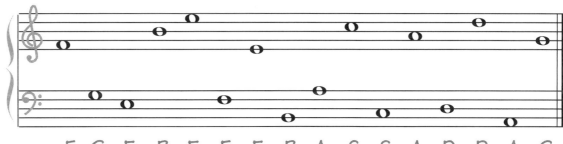

F G E B E F E B A C C A D D A G

14 Spell the words to complete the sentences below.

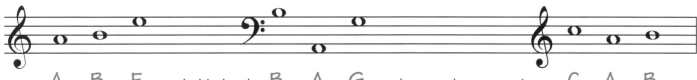

____A B E____ took his lunch ____B A G____ and went downtown in a ____C A B____ to

____F E E D____ the pigeons in the park. While eating his ____E G G____ sandwich, a ____B E E____

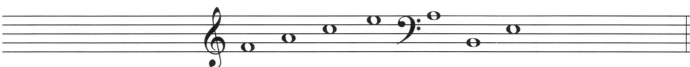

flew by and barely missed his ____F A C E____ . ____A B E____ decided to go home.

Note Values

While the placement of notes on the staff indicates the pitch, the duration of the note (how long the note is held) is determined by the note value.

A WHOLE NOTE is drawn as an open oval.

Two HALF NOTES equal the duration of one whole note.

Four QUARTER NOTES equal the duration of one whole note.

Whole Note   Half Notes   Quarter Notes

←— Stem

←— Notehead

1 Whole note = 2 Half notes = 4 Quarter notes   1 Half note = 2 Quarter notes

Stems extend *downward* on the left side when the note appears *on or above* the 3rd line of the staff.

Stems extend *upward* on the right side when the note appears *below* the 3rd line of the staff.

The stem length should continue to the space or line with the same letter name, above or below.

Stem extends to F above.   Stem extends to F below.

←— F   ←— F

Exercises

1 Fill in the blanks with the correct number:

a. __4__ ♩ = 𝅝

b. __2__ ♩ = 𝅗𝅥

c. __1__ 𝅝 = ♩♩♩♩

d. __2__ 𝅗𝅥 = 𝅝

e. __2__ 𝅗𝅥 = ♩♩♩♩

f. __1__ 𝅝 = 𝅗𝅥 𝅗𝅥

2 Draw the stems in the correct direction with the correct length. Write the names of the notes between the staff.

C   A   D   E   D   F   B   B   C   G   A

***3** Draw the treble clef and write the indicated notes. Use only notes within the staff.

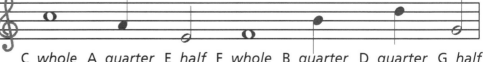

C *whole* A *quarter* E *half* F *whole* B *quarter* D *quarter* G *half*

***4** Draw the bass clef and write the indicated notes. Use only notes within the staff.

E *half* D *quarter* A *whole* C *quarter* F *half* B *whole* G *half*

*Correct student answers may vary.

Measure, Bar Line and Double Bar

Music is divided into equal parts by BAR LINES. The area between the two bar lines is called a MEASURE or BAR.

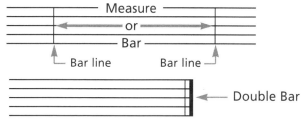

A DOUBLE BAR is written at the end of a piece of music. It is made up of one thin and one thick line, with the thick line always on the outside.

On a grand staff, the bar lines and double bar pass through the entire staff.

Exercises

1 Divide the staff below into 4 measures with a double bar at the end. A single staff does not begin with a bar line.

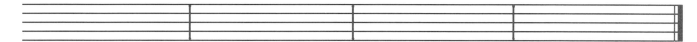

*2 Draw a treble clef. Divide the staff below into 4 measures with a double bar at the end. Write any whole note in each measure. Name the notes on the lines below the staff.

C   G   F   D

*3 Draw a bass clef. Divide the staff below into 4 measures with a double bar at the end. Write any 4 quarter notes (alternate stem direction) in each measure. Name the notes on the lines below the staff.

E A B A   D G F C   F B E G   C D D C

*4 Draw a grand staff. Divide the staff below into 4 measures with a double bar at the end. Write any two half notes in each measure (alternate stem direction and staffs). Name the notes on the lines below the staff. Begin with a bar line (before the clef signs) when there is a grand staff.

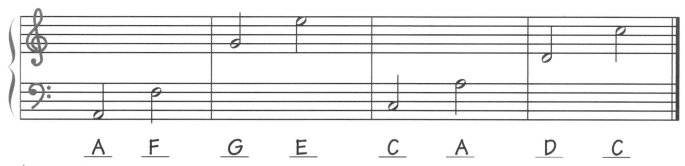

A   F   G   E   C   A   D   C

*Correct student answers may vary.

♩ Time Signature and Note Values

The TIME SIGNATURE appears at the beginning of the music after the clef sign. It contains two numbers, one above the other.

4 The upper number tells how many beats (or counts) are in each measure. In this case, 4.
4 The lower number indicates what type of note receives 1 beat. In this case, a quarter note ♩.

In ♩ time:

A quarter note (♩) is equal to one count (or beat). Count (1, 2, 3, 4) and clap the rhythm evenly (once per beat). The beat numbers are written under the notes. Also, say "ta" and clap.

A half note (♩) is equal to two counts (or beats). Count and clap the rhythm evenly (holding your hands together for 2 beats). The beat numbers are written under the notes. Also, say "ta-ah" (in a continuous sound) and clap.

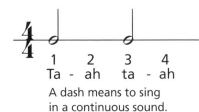

A dash means to sing in a continuous sound.

A whole note (𝅝) is equal to four counts (or beats). Count and clap the rhythm evenly (hands together for 4 beats). The beat numbers are written under the notes. Also, say "ta-ah-ah-ah" (in a continuous sound) and clap.

Exercises

1 Add the following notes to get the total number of beats:

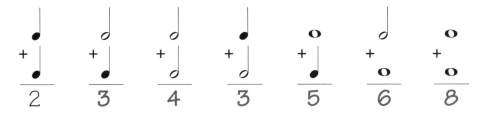

2 Draw bar lines, a double bar at the end, and stems on the appropriate notes in the following example so that there are 4 beats in each measure. Count and clap; say (using "ta", etc.) and clap.

3 Write the ♩ time signature and fill in the missing beats (if any) by adding only one note per measure. Count and clap; say and clap.

Whole, Half and Quarter Rests

Music is not only made up of sounds, but also the silence between sounds.
The duration of musical silence is determined by the value of the REST.

A WHOLE REST means to rest
for a whole measure.

It hangs down from the 4th line.

A HALF REST is equal to
half of a whole rest.

It sits on the 3rd line.

A QUARTER REST is equal to
one quarter of a whole rest.

1	2	4	1	2
Whole rest	Half rests	Quarter rests	Half rest	Quarter rests

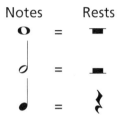

Notes   Rests

In $\frac{4}{4}$ time:

Quarter rests ⸾ are equal
to 1 beat.

1   2   3   4

Half rests ▬ are equal
to 2 beats.

1   2   3   4

Whole rests ▬ are equal
to 4 beats.

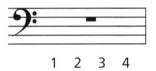

1   2   3   4

Exercises

1 Fill in the correct number:

a. __2__ ♩ = 𝅝

b. __2__ ♩ = ♩

c. __2__ ♩ = ♩♩♩♩

d. __1__ 𝅝 = ♩♩♩♩

2 Fill in the correct number:

a. __1__ ▬ = ▬ ▬

b. __2__ ▬ = ⸾ ⸾ ⸾ ⸾

c. __2__ ⸾ = ▬

d. __4__ ⸾ = ▬

3 Trace the 2nd quarter
rest, then draw 4 more.

4 Fill in the 2nd half rest,
then draw 4 more.

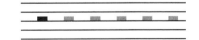

5 Fill in the 2nd whole
rest, then draw 4 more.

6   **a.** Divide the staff below into 4 measures with a double bar at the end.

    b. Add a $\frac{4}{4}$ time signature.

    c. Fill in the 1st bar with a whole rest, the 2nd bar with 2 half rests, the 3rd bar with
      4 quarter rests, the 4th bar with 1 half rest and 2 quarter rests.

Track 7

1 Listen to the following notes and rests in $\frac{4}{4}$ time.
You will hear a one measure COUNT-OFF (introduction) to indicate the TEMPO (speed) of the beat.

a. A whole note
sounds like this:

d. Quarter notes followed by
quarter rests sound like this:

b. Half notes
sound like this:

e. A half note followed by
a half rest sounds like this:

c. Quarter notes
sound like this:

f. A whole note followed by
a whole rest sounds like this:

Track 8

2 Listen to the following example in $\frac{4}{4}$ time. There will be a 4-beat count-off.

Dreydl, Dreydl

Traditional Hanukkah Song

Track 9

3 One example will be played for each exercise.
Circle the example played.

a.

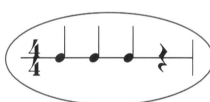

b.
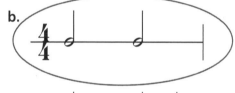

c.

Track 10

4 You will hear two
examples played for
each exercise. Determine
which rhythm played
matches the one written.
Circle the number to the
right of the staff.

a.

b.

Track 11

5 Write the rhythm of the following two bar examples using the note A.
Each example will be played twice.

a.

b.

Fill in the correct number:

1 __2__ 𝅗𝅥 = 𝅝   **2** __4__ 𝅘𝅥 = 𝅝   **3** __1__ 𝅗𝅥 = 𝅘𝅥 𝅘𝅥

4 The duration of a 𝅗𝅥 is (circle one)

(longer) or **shorter** than a 𝅘𝅥.

5 When the notes are written on or above the 3rd line of the staff, stems extend (circle one) **upward** or (downward) on the left side of the notehead.

6 Music is divided into equal parts by __bar lines_____.

7 A __double bar_____ is written at the end of a piece of music.

8 The upper number of the time signature indicates how many __beats__ are in each measure.

The bottom number of the time signature indicates what type of note receives __1__ beat.

9 When a time signature contains a 4 as the top number, it means __4__ beats in each measure.

When a time signature contains a 4 as the bottom number, it means a __quarter__ note receives __1__ beat.

10 ▬ is called a __half__ __rest__. In ⁴⁄₄ time, rest for __2__ beats.

▬ is called a __whole__ __rest__. In ⁴⁄₄ time, rest for __4__ beats.

𝄽 is called a __quarter__ __rest__. In ⁴⁄₄ time, rest for __1__ beat.

11 Draw 4 quarter rests on the staff: Draw 2 half rests on the staff: Draw 1 whole rest on the staff:

12 In the example below, draw a treble clef and ⁴⁄₄ time signature. Add the stems where necessary and write the beats under the notes.

Au Claire de la Lune   French Folk Song

1 2 3 4   1 2 3 4   1 2 3 4   1 2 3 4   1 2 3 4   1 2 3 4   1 2 3 4   1 2 3 4

13 Add bar lines and a double bar to the example below. Count and clap; say and clap. Write the names of the notes below the staff.

Hatikvah   Israeli National Anthem

A B C D   E E   F E F A   E   D D D   C C   B A B C   A

14 Fill in the missing beats with notes in the 2nd space by adding only one note in each measure.

a.
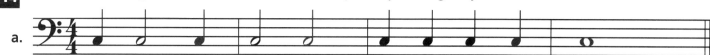

Fill in the missing beats with rests by adding only one rest in each measure.

b.

$\frac{2}{4}$ *Time Signature*

In $\frac{2}{4}$ time: $\mathbf{\frac{2}{4}}$ means there are 2 beats per measure.

means the quarter note ♩ receives 1 beat.

$\frac{2}{4}$ and $\frac{4}{4}$ both have 4 as the bottom number, meaning a quarter note ♩ receives 1 beat.
The difference is that $\frac{2}{4}$ has 2 beats per measure while $\frac{4}{4}$ has 4.

In $\frac{2}{4}$ time: ♩ or 𝄽 = 1 beat

♩ or ▬ = 2 beats*

Count: 1 2   1 2   1 2   1 2

*A whole rest ▬ is used for a full measure of rest, even if there are only 2 beats in each measure.
In writing music, a half rest and a whole note are never used in $\frac{2}{4}$ time.

Exercises

* 1 Complete the measures using notes and rests. Count and clap.

1 2   1 2   1 2   1 2   1 2   1 2

2 Circle the measures with the incorrect number of beats.

3 Draw bar lines and a double bar in the correct places. Count and clap.

4 Rewrite the $\frac{4}{4}$ music line in $\frac{2}{4}$ on the staff below. Write the names of the notes below the staff.

G G   A A   D   B   G G   A A   D B   G

*Correct student answers may vary.

¾ *Time Signature*

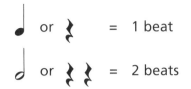 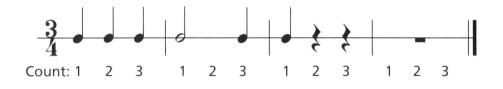

In ¾ time: means there are 3 beats per measure.

means the quarter note ♩ receives 1 beat.

♩ or 𝄽 = 1 beat

♩ or 𝄽 𝄽 = 2 beats   Count: 1 2 3   1 2 3   1 2 3   1 2 3

A whole rest ▬ is used for a full measure of rest, even if there are only 3 beats in each measure.
In writing music, a half rest and a whole note are never used in ¾ time.

¾, ¾ and ⁴⁄₄ all have 4 as the bottom number, meaning the quarter note ♩ always receives 1 beat.

The difference is that:

²⁄₄ has 2 beats per measure.   ¾ has 3 beats per measure.   ⁴⁄₄ has 4 beats per measure.

Exercises

1 Complete the measures using one note or rest. Count and clap.

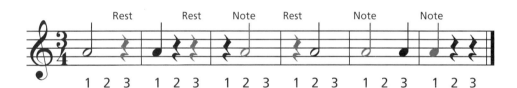

1 2 3   1 2 3   1 2 3   1 2 3   1 2 3   1 2 3

2 Circle the measures with the incorrect number of beats.

3 In the example below, draw bar lines and a double bar in the correct places. Count and clap.

4 In the exercise below:
   a. Add the note stems, bar lines and a double bar. Add whole rests where appropriate.
   b. Write the beats below the grand staff, then count and clap.
   c. Write the names of the notes below the beats.

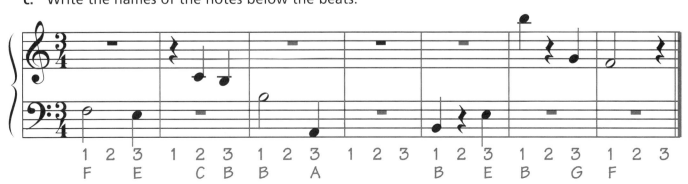

1 2 3   1 2 3   1 2 3   1 2 3   1 2 3   1 2 3   1 2 3
F   E   C B B   A   B   E B   G   F

Dotted Half Note

A dot after a note increases its duration by half the original value: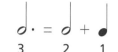

Count: 1 2   1 2 3
Say: Ta-ah   ta-ah-ah

In $\frac{3}{4}$ and $\frac{4}{4}$, a half note receives two beats.
Because a dot following a half note increases its duration by 1 beat,
a dotted half note has a value of 3 beats.

Count and clap the rhythm:
Say and clap the rhythm:

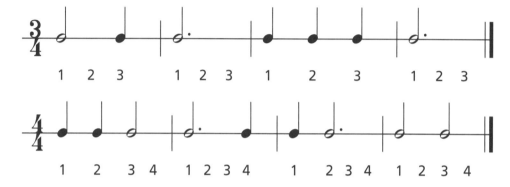

Exercises

1 Write one note equal in value to the sum of the notes or rests.

a. ♩ + 𝅗𝅥 = 𝅗𝅥.

b. 𝅗𝅥. + ♩ = 𝅝

c. 𝄽 + ▬ = 𝅗𝅥.

d. 𝄽 + 𝄽 = 𝅗𝅥

2 Write the number of beats remaining for each example.

a. 𝅗𝅥. – 𝅗𝅥 = 1

b. 𝅗𝅥. – ♩ = 2

c. 𝅝 – ♩ = 3

d. 𝅝 – ▬ = 2

3 Complete the measures using one note or rest. Count and clap.

a.

b.

4 In the example below:
  a. Draw the grand staff.
  b. Add the note stems, bar lines and a double bar.
  c. Write the names of the notes below the grand staff.

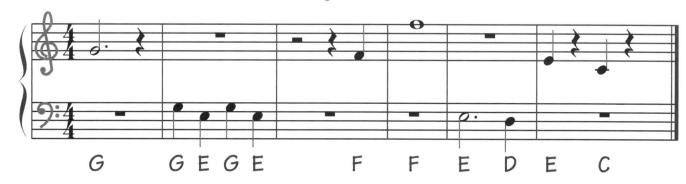

G   G E G E   F   F E D E C

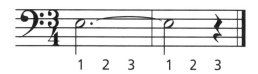

Ties and Slurs

A TIE *joins* two notes of the *same* pitch by a curved line over or under the notes.
Each note joined by a tie is held for its full value but only the first note is played or sung.
The tied note's value is added to the value of the first note.

The TIE should always be written on the opposite side from the note stems.

A SLUR *smoothly connects* two or more notes of *different* pitches by a curved line over or under the notes. There is no break in sound between pitches. This is also referred to as LEGATO playing or singing.

Aura Lee   American Folk Song

On wind instruments, only the first note of a group of slurred notes should be tongued.

On string instruments, a slur indicates a group of notes to be played in one bow.

On keyboard instruments, slurs indicate when to lift the hands.

When all of the stems are in the same direction, the slur is written on the side opposite from that of the stems. When stem direction is mixed, the slur is written *above* the notes.

Exercises

1 Write the note that equals the tied notes.

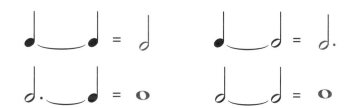

2 Write the number of beats in each example.

3 In each example, mark an "S" or "T" to indicate whether the musical passage is made up of tied or slurred notes.

4 Write a slur or tie in each example and mark an "S" or "T" below.

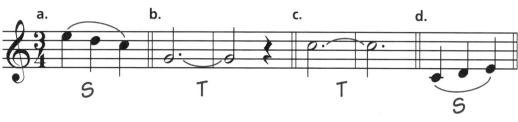

Track 12

1 Listen to the following examples in $\frac{2}{4}$ time. You will hear a one measure count-off.

a. Quarter notes sound like this:

b. Quarter notes followed by quarter rests sound like this:

c. Half notes sound like this:

  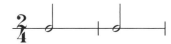

Track 13

2 Listen and follow the rhythm of the example below.

What is the curved line in measures 1 and 2 called? __slur__ In measures 4–5, 5–6, 6–7? __tie__

Track 14

3 In the measures below, listen to the rhythm pattern. Write the missing rhythm in the 3rd measure using the note F. Each example will be played twice.

a.

b.

Track 15

4 Listen to the examples in $\frac{3}{4}$ time. You will hear a one measure count-off.

a. Quarter notes sound like this:

b. Half notes followed by quarter rests sound like this:

c. Dotted half notes sound like this:

Track 16

5 Listen and follow the rhythm of the example below.

Take Me Out to the Ball Game   Albert von Tilzer (1873–1956)

What is the curved line in measures 3–4 called? __slur__ In measures 7–8? __tie__

Track 17

6 Write the rhythm of the following two bar examples using the note A. Each example will be played twice.

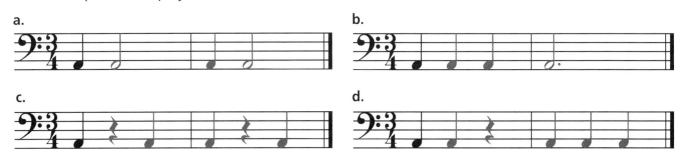

a.

b.

c.

d.

Fill in the blanks:

1 In ²₄, ³₄ and ⁴₄ time, the ___quarter___ note receives one beat.

2 In ²₄ time, there are __2__ beats per measure.

3 In ³₄ time, there are __3__ beats per measure.

4 In ³₄ time, a dotted half note receives __3__ beats.

5 In ⁴₄ time, a dotted half note receives __3__ beats.

6 In ²₄ time, a whole rest receives __2__ beats.

7 In ³₄ time, a whole rest receives __3__ beats.

8 In ⁴₄ time, a whole rest receives __4__ beats.

9 Legato singing or playing means to play the music __smoothly__ __connected__

10 On wind instruments, only the first note of a group of __slurred__ notes should be tongued.

11 A slur occurs when 2 or more notes of (circle one) **the same** or (different) pitch(es) are joined by a curved line.

12 A tie occurs when 2 notes of (circle one) (the same) or **different** pitch(es) are joined by a curved line.

13 Draw an X above the note where you would change direction of the bow on a string instrument. Write the names of the notes below the staff.

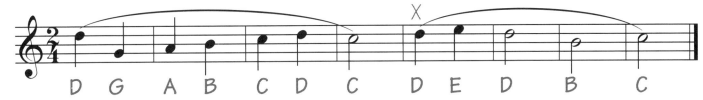

D G A B C D C D E D B C

14 Draw an X above the notes where you would tongue on a wind instrument. Write the names of the notes below the staff.

A B A B C B C D B A

15 Draw an X before the notes where you would lift the hand on a keyboard instrument. Write the names of the notes below the staff.

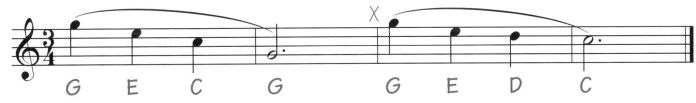

G E C G G E D C

16 Write the number of beats in each example on the line.

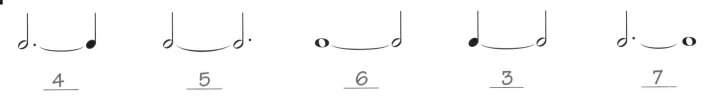

4   5   6   3   7

17 Write the correct time signature in the appropriate place and the beats below the staff.

a.    b.    c.

Repeat Sign, 1st and 2nd Endings

Two dots placed *before* the double bar ⁚‖ indicates a REPEAT SIGN.
It means to go back to the beginning and play or sing the music again.

Go back to the beginning and repeat.

Repeat signs sometimes appear in pairs *within* a piece of music. ‖⁚ ⁚‖
The first repeat sign will then have the two dots placed *after* the double bar.
When this occurs, return to the first repeat sign at the beginning of the section.

Go back to ‖⁚ and repeat.

Another way of indicating a repeat is with 1st and 2nd endings. Play or sing through the 1st ending to the repeat sign, then go back to the beginning. When repeating, skip the 1st ending and play the 2nd.

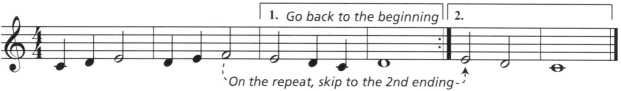

1. Go back to the beginning 2.

On the repeat, skip to the 2nd ending

Exercises

1 Rewrite the following example using a repeat sign.

2 Rewrite the following example using a pair of repeat signs.

3 Rewrite the following example using 1st and 2nd endings.

Camptown Races   Stephen Foster (1826–1864)

Eighth Notes

When you add a flag to the stem of a quarter note, it becomes an EIGHTH NOTE ♪

Two or more 8th notes are connected by a beam

In $\frac{2}{4}$, $\frac{3}{4}$ and $\frac{4}{4}$ time: 8th notes are equal to one-half count. For two 8th notes, count "1 &" or say "ti ti."

Two 8th notes equal 1 quarter note.

Four 8th notes equal 1 half note.

Eight 8th notes equal 1 whole note.

1 & 1
ti ti

1 & 2 & 1 2
ti ti ti ti

1 & 2 & 3 & 4 & 1 2 3 4
ti ti ti ti ti ti ti ti

Eighth notes can be drawn:

1. As a single quarter note with a flag attached to the stem,

2. or with a beam, in pairs

or in fours.

Write eight single 8th notes (4 with stems up, 4 with stems down).

Write two sets of beamed 8th notes (1 with stems up, 1 with stems down), in pairs and in fours.

Exercises

1 Add stems with flags or beams to make 8th notes as indicated.

Flags   2 sets in pairs   Flags   1 set in four

2 Fill in the correct number:

a. __2__

b. __4__

c. __6__

d. __8__

3 Write one note equal to the value of the notes preceding it.

a.

b.

c.

d.

4 Complete the measures below using beamed 8th notes.

1 & 2 & 3 & 4 &   1 & 2 & 3 & 4 &   1 & 2 & 3 & 4 &   1 & 2 & 3 & 4 &   1 & 2 & 3 & 4 &

Eighth Rests

An EIGHTH REST ⅞ is equal to half the value of a quarter rest ⸓. In $\frac{2}{4}$, $\frac{3}{4}$ and $\frac{4}{4}$ time:

Two 8th rests equal 1 quarter rest.	Four 8th rests equal 1 half rest.	Eight 8th rests equal 1 whole rest.

Trace along the dotted lines to draw an 8th rest, then draw 8 more.

Notes or rests on beats 1, 2, 3 or 4 are considered *on the beat*. When tapping your toe evenly, the beat is when your toe touches the floor. Notes or rests on the "&" are considered *off the beat* or *up-beat*.

Count: 1 & 2 & 3 & 4 &

on the   off the
beat   beat

Exercises

1   Clap the following rhythm, counting aloud.

2   Fill in the correct number:

   a. __4__ ⅞ rests = ▬   b. __2__ ⅞ rests = ⸓

   c. __8__ ⅞ rests = ▬ ($\frac{4}{4}$ time)   d. __6__ ⅞ rests = ▬ + ⸓

3   Change these quarter notes to single 8th notes, then add 8th rests between them.

4   Write the beats (1 & 2 &) under the notes. On the line below, write whether the 8th rest occurs "on" or "off" the beat.

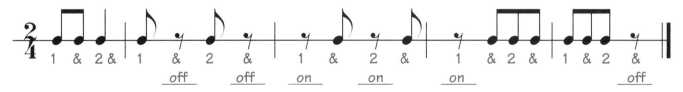

5   Complete the measures below by adding only one rest per measure. Write the beats (1 & 2 & 3 & 4 &) under the notes and rests, then clap the rhythm.

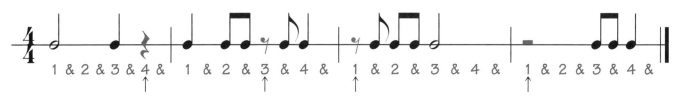

Dotted Quarter Note

Remember: a dot after a note increases
its duration by half the original value.

In $\frac{2}{4}$, $\frac{3}{4}$ and $\frac{4}{4}$, a quarter note receives one beat. Because a
dot following a quarter note increases its duration by ½ beat,
a dotted quarter note has a value of 1½ beats.

A ♩. is usually followed by an ♪

Clap and count the rhythm.

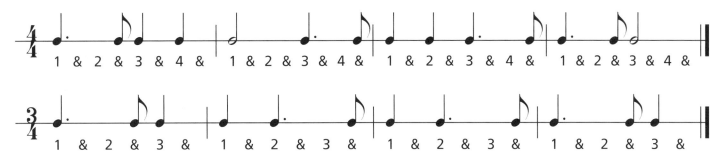

Exercises

1 Write the beats under the following example. Count and clap.

Alouette   French-Canadian Folk Song

2 Fill in the blanks with
the correct number: a. ___1___ ♩. = ♪♪♪♪   b. ___2___ ♩. = ♩♩♩   c. ___1___ ♩. = ♩♪

3 Add bar lines to the examples below.

a.

b.

4 Complete the measures using only one note or rest—alternate notes and rests.

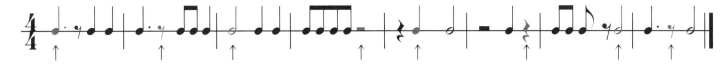

UNIT 4   EAR TRAINING FOR LESSONS 14–17

Track 18

1 In each time signature, there are natural strong beats. In $\frac{2}{4}$ time, the strong beat is on beat one. Listen to the example below in $\frac{2}{4}$ time.

El Capitan   John Philip Sousa (1854–1932)

Track 19

2 In $\frac{3}{4}$ time, the strong beat is on beat one. Listen to the example below in $\frac{3}{4}$ time.

Symphony No. 8, Op. 93   Ludwig van Beethoven (1770–1827)

Track 20

3 In $\frac{4}{4}$ time, the strong beat is on beat one, with a secondary emphasis on beat three. Listen to the example below in $\frac{4}{4}$ time.

Trumpet Voluntary   Jeremiah Clarke (c. 1673–1707)

Track 21

4 In the two examples below, listen for the ♩. ♪ rhythm.

Hallelujah Chorus (from "Messiah")   George Frideric Handel (1685–1759)

a.

All Through the Night   Welsh Folk Song

b.

Track 22

5 Listen to the 2 measure example and write the rhythm.
The example will be played twice.

Track 23

6 Listen to the 4 measure example and write the rhythm.
The example will be played twice.

1 Repeat signs are two dots before or after a <u>double bar</u>.

2 How many total measures would a musician play in the following example? <u>8</u>

Anvil Chorus (from "Il Trovatore")   Giuseppe Verdi (1813–1901)

3 Fill in the correct number: a. <u>4</u> ♪ = 𝅗𝅥   b. <u>6</u> ♪ = 𝅗𝅥·   c. <u>3</u> ♪ = ♩·   d. <u>8</u> ♪ = 𝅝

4 Complete the notes by adding stems to the first measure and beamed notes (in pairs) to the second measure. Be sure the stems are pointing in the correct direction.

5 Fill in the correct number: a. <u>4</u> 𝄾 = ▬   b. <u>6</u> 𝄾 = 𝄽 ▬   c. <u>2</u> 𝄾 = 𝄽   d. <u>8</u> 𝄾 = ▬ (4/4)

6 Complete the measures by adding one rest above each arrow.

Hallelujah Chorus (from "Messiah")   George Frideric Handel (1685–1759)

7 ♩· = <u>1½</u> beats in 2/4, 3/4 and 4/4 time.

8 Rewrite the example using 1st and 2nd endings in the staff below.

Minuet   Johann Sebastian Bach (1685–1750)

Dynamic Signs

DYNAMIC SIGNS indicate the volume, or how *soft* or *loud* the music should be played. Most musical terms are written in Italian since Italian composers were among the first to write such instructions in their manuscripts.

The word *piano* in Italian means soft; the word *forte* means loud.
The most commonly used dynamic signs are:

ITALIAN	SIGN	ENGLISH
piano	p	soft
forte	f	loud
mezzo piano	mp	moderately soft
mezzo forte	mf	moderately loud
pianissimo	pp	very soft
fortissimo	ff	very loud

Mezzo means moderately; *issimo* means very.
Dynamic signs arranged in order from very soft to very loud, are: pp, p, mp, mf, f, ff

A Gradual Change in Dynamics
Terms used to indicate a gradual change in volume,
from *soft* to *loud* or *loud* to *soft* are:

ITALIAN	SIGN	ENGLISH
crescendo or **cresc.**	$\diagup$	gradually louder
diminuendo or **dim.** or **decrescendo** or **decresc.**	$\diagdown$	gradually softer

Exercises

1 Write the Italian word for the following dynamic signs:

f _forte_ pp _pianissimo_

mp _mezzo piano_ ff _fortissimo_

$\diagdown$ _decrescendo_ mf _mezzo forte_

p _piano_ $\diagup$ _crescendo_

2 Clap the following line, observing the dynamic signs indicated.

3 Use every dynamic sign learned above at least once to mark the appropriate dynamic signs on the lines beneath the following story.

"Wake up!" whispered Ron to his brother Steven. The boys walked softly out the door. They heard

a. _pp_   b. _p_

the moderately soft sound of a distant airplane, which became gradually louder and roared very loudly as it

c. _mp_   d. _⟋_   e. _ff_

flew over head, then faded away gradually. Steven said, "Let's play basketball," in a

f. _⟍_

moderately loud voice. They shouted a loud "Yes!" as they ran to the park.

g. _mf_   h. _f_

Tempo Marks

TEMPO is an Italian word meaning "rate of speed." Tempo marks tell how *fast* or *slow* the music should be played. Tempo marks are also written in Italian.

ITALIAN	ENGLISH
Largo	Very slow
Adagio	Slow
Andante	Moving along (walking speed)
Moderato	Moderately
Allegro	Quickly, cheerfully
Vivace	Lively and fast

Moderato may be combined with other words:

Allegro moderato = slightly slower than *Allegro* but quicker than *Moderato*

A Gradual Change of Tempo
Terms used to indicate a gradual change in tempo are:

ITALIAN	TERM	ENGLISH
ritardando	*ritard.* or *rit.*	gradually slower
accelerando	*accel.*	gradually faster

Exercises

1 In writing music, tempo marks tell the ___rate___ ___of___ ___speed___.

2 A very slow tempo marking is ___Largo___.

3 A lively and fast tempo marking is ___Vivace___.

4 Match the Italian term to its English meaning by writing the correct letter in each blank.

_h_	Quickly, cheerfully	a.	*Moderato*
_d_	Gradually slower	b.	*Vivace*
_b_	Lively and fast	c.	*Adagio*
_a_	Moderately	d.	*Ritardando*
_g_	Moving along (walking speed)	e.	*Accelerando*
_f_	Very slow	f.	*Largo*
_e_	Gradually faster	g.	*Andante*
_c_	Slow	h.	*Allegro*

Articulation

Pages 28 and 29 introduced the words and signs that indicate what speed (slow to fast) and volume (soft to loud) a musical selection is to be played. In addition, notes may be performed in different ways. The manner in which a note is performed is called ARTICULATION. Legato (see page 19) is one form of articulation.

ITALIAN	SYMBOL	ENGLISH
staccato		Play the note short and detached. The Italian word means "detached."
accent (English)	>	Play the note louder, with a special emphasis.
sforzando	*sf* or *sfz*	A sudden, strong accent. The Italian word means "forcing."
tenuto	(or **ten.**)	Hold the note for its full value. The Italian word means "held."
fermata		Hold the note longer than its normal value (approximately twice the normal duration).

Exercises

1 Name the articulation symbols below:

♩ _____ staccato _____   ♩ or **ten.** _____ tenuto _____

> _____ accent _____   *sf* or *sfz* _____ sforzando _____

⌢ _____ fermata _____

2 Say the following examples using the syllables "ti" for 8th notes, "ta" for quarter notes, "ta-ah" for half notes, "ta-ah-ah" for dotted half notes and "ta-ah-ah-ah" for whole notes. Observe all tempo markings, dynamics and other musical symbols.

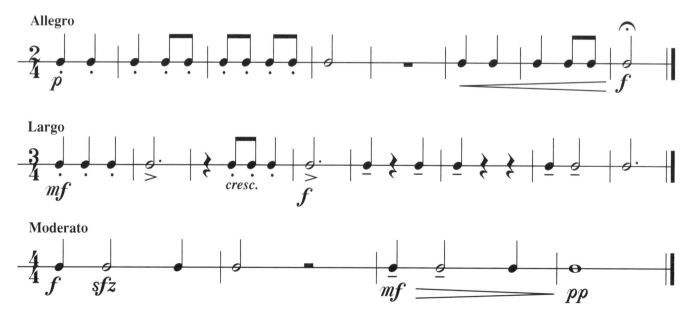

D.C., D.S., Coda and Fine

To reduce the amount of music needed to notate a piece, several additional Italian words and symbols are used by composers to indicate repeats.

ITALIAN	SIGN	ENGLISH
Da Capo	*D.C.*	Repeat from the beginning
Dal Segno	*D.S.*	Repeat from the sign 𝄋
Fine	*Fine*	The end
Coda*	⊕	An added ending

*When the Coda sign appears in the music, it means to skip directly
to the Coda, which is an added ending usually marked with the same sign.

The Italian words and symbols for repeating are frequently combined.

SIGN **ENGLISH**
D.C. al Fine Repeat from the beginning and play to the end (Fine).

1. *Play through to the end* 2. *Return to the beginning* 3. *Play to Fine*

D.S. al Fine Repeat from the sign 𝄋 and play to the end (Fine).

1. *Play through to the end* 2. *Return to 𝄋* 3. *Play to Fine*

D.C. al Coda Repeat from the beginning and play to ⊕, then skip to the ⊕ Coda.

1. *Play to D.C. al Coda* 2. *Return to the beginning* 3. *Play to ⊕* 4. *Skip to ⊕ Coda and play to the end.*

D.S. al Coda Repeat from 𝄋 and play to ⊕, then skip to the ⊕ Coda

1. *Play to D.S. al Coda* 2. *Return to 𝄋* 3. *Play to ⊕* 4. *Skip to ⊕ Coda and play to the end.*

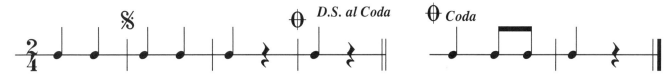

UNIT 5 EAR TRAINING FOR LESSONS 18–21

Track 24

1 Listen to the example and place the
following dynamic markings where applicable: *f* , *mf* , *ff*

Symphony No. 9 ("From the New World"), Op. 95

Antonin Dvořák (1841–1904)

2 In the example above, circle the appropriate tempo marking: **Largo**   (**Allegro**)   **Andante**

Track 25

3 Listen to the example and notate where the *ritardando (rit.)* and *accelerando (accel.)* occur.

Track 26

4 Listen to the example and place the
following markings in the appropriate places: Fermata (⌢)   Sforzando (*sfz*)

Track 27

5 Listen to the example and mark accents (>) under the notes that are played accented.

Rondo Alla Turca (from "Sonata in A Major, K. 331")

Wolfgang Amadeus Mozart (1756–1791)

6 In the example above, circle the appropriate tempo marking: **Vivace**   **Adagio**   (**Moderato**)

Track 28

7 Listen to the example and write staccato (·) marks under the appropriate quarter notes.

Shepherd's Hey

English Folk Song

Track 29

8 Listen to the example and place the following two markings
in the appropriate places: *sfz*   ⟍

1   Arrange the following dynamics in order from softest to loudest to softest: *mf , pp , f , mp , p , ff* .

   pp   *p*   *mp*   *mf*   *f*   *ff*   *f*   *mf*   *mp*   *p*   *pp*

2   *Mezzo* (*m*) means _____moderately_____ .   **3** *issimo* means _____very_____ .

4   **Crescendo (cresc.)** means __gradually__ __louder__ .

5   **Diminuendo (dim.)** or **decrescendo (decresc.)** means __gradually__ __softer__ .

6   Arrange the following tempo marks in order from slowest to fastest:

     Andante, Vivace, Adagio, Allegro, Moderato, Largo.

   Largo   Adagio   Andante   Moderato   Allegro   Vivace

Slowest ·· ➤ *Fastest*

7   **Allegro moderato** means slightly slower than __Allegro__ but quicker than __Moderato__ .

8   **Ritardando (ritard. or rit.)** means __gradually__ __slower__ .

9   **Accelerando (accel.)** means __gradually__ __faster__ .

10   Staccato means __short and detached__ .   **11** Tenuto means to __hold note full value__ .

12   The sign that means to hold a note for longer than its normal value is _____⌢· _____ .

13   Write the word for each symbol:

    a. ♩· _____staccato_____   b. > _____accent_____

    c. *sfz* _____sforzando_____   d. ♩‿ _____tenuto_____

14   The sign that indicates to repeat from the beginning and play to the end is _____D.C. al Fine_____ .

15   The sign that indicates to repeat from the 𝄋 and play to the end is _____D.S. al Fine_____ .

16   What is the term used to identify a separate section that ends a piece of music? _____Coda_____ .

17   Write the following musical example as it would actually be played without the *D.C. al Fine* or *Fine*.

Flats

The FLAT sign (♭) before a note lowers the pitch of that note. On the keyboard, play the next key to the left, whether black or white.

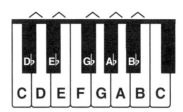

When speaking of flatted notes, the word "flat" comes after the letter name, as in **A flat**. However, in written music, the flat sign comes before the note.

A flat

To draw a flat sign, first draw a vertical line:

then add the heavier curved line:

When a flat sign is attached to a line note, the flat is centered on the line.

Add flat signs to the line notes below.

When a flat sign is attached to a space note, the flat is centered in the space.

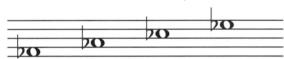

Add flat signs to the space notes below.

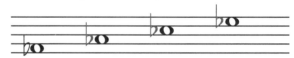

Exercises

1 In the example, write flat signs before each note, then name the notes.

2 Write the names of the piano keys in the boxes.

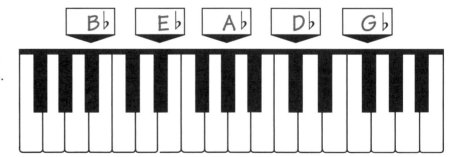

* **3** Write a treble clef and the notes indicated on the staff using half notes.

* **4** Write a bass clef and the notes indicated on the staff using quarter notes.

*Correct student answers may vary.

Sharps

The SHARP sign (♯) before a note raises the pitch of that note. On the keyboard, play the next key to the right, whether black or white.

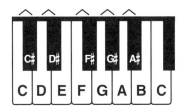

When speaking of sharped notes, the word "sharp" comes after the letter name, as in **C sharp**. However, in written music, the sharp sign comes before the note.

C sharp

To draw a sharp sign, first draw two vertical lines:

then add the heavier slanting lines:

When a sharp sign is attached to a line note, the sharp is centered on the line.

Add sharp signs to the line notes below.

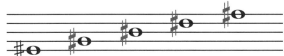

When a sharp sign is attached to a space note, the sharp is centered in the space.

Add sharp signs to the space notes below.

Exercises

1 In the example, write sharp signs before each note, then name the notes.

F# C# G# A# D# F# E# E# B#

2 Write the names of the piano keys in the boxes.

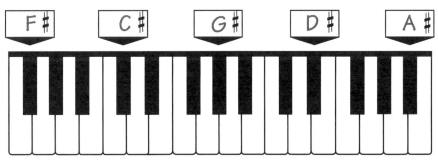

3 Write a treble clef and the notes indicated on the staff using single 8th notes.

Naturals

The NATURAL sign (♮) before a note cancels a previous sharp or flat.
On the keyboard, a note after a natural is *always* a white key.

When speaking of natural notes, the word "natural" comes after the letter name, as in **B natural**. However, in written music, the natural sign comes before the note.

B natural

To draw a natural sign, first draw the left half:

then draw the right half:

When a natural sign is attached to a line note, the natural is centered on the line.

Add natural signs to the line notes below.

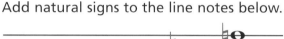

When a natural sign is attached to a space note, the natural is centered in the space.

Add natural signs to the space notes below.

When ♭, ♯ or ♮ signs appear within a musical piece, they are called ACCIDENTALS.
An accidental sign affects the notes written on the same line or space following it *for that measure only*.

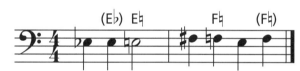

A bar line cancels all accidentals in the previous measure, except if a note is tied across the bar line.

Exercises

1 In the example, write natural signs before each note, then name the notes.

E   B   G   G   D   A   C   F   A

2 Write the names of the notes on the lines below the staff.

Circus March (from "Entry of the Gladiators")   Julius Fučik (1872–1916)

C   B   A#   B   A#   A♮   A♭   G   F#   G   A   A♭   G   A♭   G   F#   F♮   E   D#   E

Whole Steps, Half Steps and Enharmonic Notes

The distance from any key on the keyboard to the very next key above or below, whether black or white, is a HALF STEP (H).

The distance from any key to two keys above or below, is a WHOLE STEP (W).

The key a half step up from C is C♯. This key is also a half step down from D, and is also known as D♭.

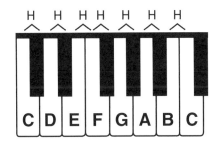

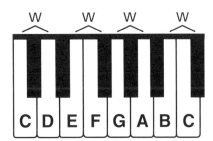

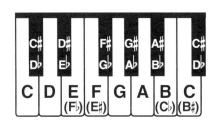

Many notes sound the same but are written differently. These notes are called ENHARMONIC NOTES.

Exercises

1 The enharmonic note for F♭ is ___E___. The enharmonic note for E♯ is ___F___.

The enharmonic note for C♭ is ___B___. The enharmonic note for B♯ is ___C___.

2 Write the 2 indicated enharmonic notes on the staff and name the notes in the spaces below:
  a. one half step above G
  b. one half step below F
  c. one half step below B
  d. one half step above D

a. _G#_ _Ab_   **b.** _Fb_ _E_   **c.** _Bb_ _A#_   **d.** _D#_ _Eb_

3 Write the indicated notes on the staff and the name of the note in the spaces below. If there are enharmonic notes, write both.
  a. one whole step above G♯
  b. one whole step below F
  c. one whole step below A
  d. one whole step above E

a. _A#_ _Bb_   **b.** _Eb_ _D#_   **c.** _G_   **d.** _F#_ _Gb_

4 Name the notes and indicate whether the distance between each pair of notes is a whole step (W) or a half step (H).

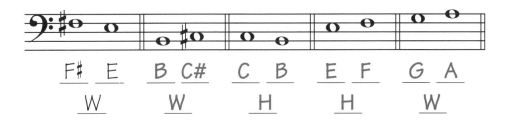

F♯   E   B   C♯   C   B   E   F   G   A
  W   W   H   H   W

UNIT 6   EAR TRAINING FOR LESSONS 22–25

Track 30

1 In each example, you will hear two notes.
If the 2nd note is a half step below, draw a flat (♭) in front of it.

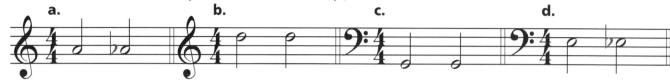

Track 31

2 In each example, you will hear a short musical phrase. Circle the phrase that you hear.

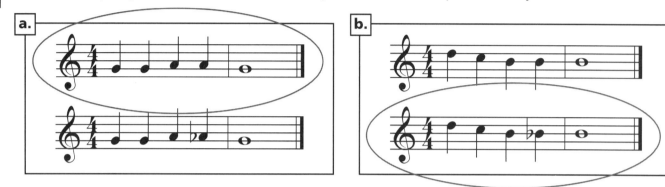

Track 32

3 In each example, you will hear two notes. If the 2nd note is a half step above, draw a sharp (♯) in front of it.

Track 33

4 You will hear a half step that moves up or down.
If the 2nd note moves up a half step, draw a sharp (♯) in front of it.
If the 2nd note moves down a half step, draw a flat (♭) in front of it.

Track 34

5 You will hear a whole step that moves *up* or *down*. Draw the 2nd note on the staff using a half note.

Track 35

6 In the following example, draw the missing notes in the boxes.

March Slav

Moderato   Peter Ilyich Tchaikovsky (1840–1893)

1 Circle one: The flat sign (♭) **raises** or (lowers) the pitch.

2 Circle one: The sharp sign (♯) (raises) or **lowers** the pitch.

3 A natural sign _cancels_ a previous sharp or flat.

4 An accidental is in effect for ___1___ measure(s) only.

5 Write the following notes on the staff below. Write the notes in two places, one above the other.

6 The note F is ___1___ half step(s) above E.

7 The note D is ___1___ whole step(s) above C.

8 The note F is ___1___ whole step(s) below G.

9 *Name 2 notes that are a half step away from A. ___Ab___ ___G#___.

10 The enharmonic note for:

E♯ is ___F___.

B♯ is ___C___.

F♭ is ___E___.

C♭ is ___B___.

*Correct student answers may vary.

Music Crossword

Fill in the boxes with the correct answers. Do not leave a space between words.

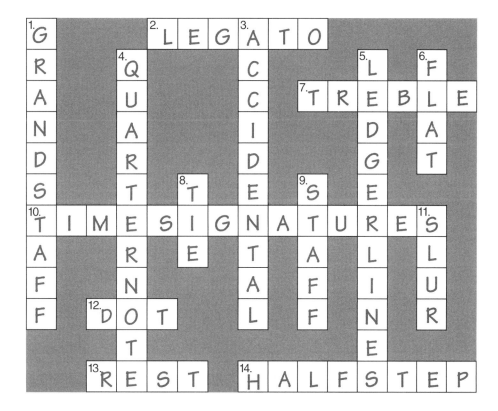

ACROSS

2. Smoothly connected
7. The name of the staff used for higher pitches
10. $\frac{2}{4}$, $\frac{3}{4}$, $\frac{4}{4}$
12. This symbol increases the value of the note by half
13. Musical silence
14. On a keyboard, the distance from one key to the next key (either right or left)

DOWN

1. Treble and Bass staffs together
3. Flat, Sharp or Natural
4. What receives one beat in $\frac{3}{4}$ time
5. Lines added to a staff to extend the range
6. Lowers the pitch by a half step
8. Curved line connecting 2 or more notes of the same pitch
9. 5 lines and the spaces between
11. Curved line connecting 2 or more notes of different pitches

GLOSSARY & INDEX OF TERMS & SYMBOLS

Includes all the terms and symbols used in Book 1 and the page on which they are first introduced.

ACCELERANDO (accel.) Gradually faster (p. 29).

ACCENT > Play the note louder, with a special emphasis (p. 30).

ACCIDENTAL ♭ ♯ ♮ A flat, sharp or natural sign that appears within a piece of music. An accidental sign affects the notes written on the same line or space following it for that measure only (p. 36).

ADAGIO Slow (p. 29).

ALLEGRO Quickly, cheerfully (p. 29).

ANDANTE Moving along (walking speed) (p. 29).

ARTICULATION The manner in which a note is performed (p. 30).

BAR LINE The lines which cross the staff and divide it into measures or bars (p. 11).

BASS (or F) CLEF ✆: The clef used for notes in the lower pitch ranges (p. 5).

BASS STAFF The staff on which the bass clef is placed. The two dots of the clef surround the line on which the note F is placed (p. 5).

CLEF A sign that helps organize the 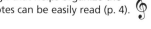 staff so notes can be easily read (p. 4).

CODA ⊕ An added ending (p. 31).

COUNT-OFF The introduction given before a piece of music is performed to indicate the tempo of the beat (p. 14).

CRESCENDO (cresc.) ◁ Gradually louder (p. 28).

D.C. (DA CAPO) Repeat from the beginning (p. 31).

D.C. al CODA Repeat from the beginning and play to ⊕, then skip to the ⊕ Coda (p. 31).

D.C. al FINE Repeat from the beginning and play to the end (Fine) (p. 31).

DECRESCENDO (decresc.) ▷ Gradually softer (p. 28).

DIMINUENDO (dim.) ▷ Gradually softer (p. 28).

DOT AFTER A NOTE ♩. Increases the note's duration by half the original value (p. 18).

DOTTED HALF NOTE ♩. In ¾ and ⁴⁄₄ time signatures, it receives 3 beats (p. 18).

DOTTED QUARTER NOTE ♩. In time signatures with 4 as the bottom number, it receives 1½ beats (p. 25).

DOUBLE BAR ‖ Is written at the end of a piece of music (p. 11).

D.S. (DAL SEGNO) Repeat from the sign 𝄋 (p. 31).

D.S. al CODA Repeat from the sign 𝄋 and play to ⊕, then skip to the ⊕ Coda (p. 31).

D.S. al FINE Repeat from the sign 𝄋 and play to the end (Fine) (p. 31).

DYNAMIC SIGNS Indicate the volume, or how soft or loud the music should be played (p. 28).

EIGHTH NOTE ♪ ♫ In time signatures with 4 as the bottom number, it receives ½ beat (p. 23).

EIGHTH REST ♪ In time signatures with 4 as the bottom number, it receives ½ beat of silence (p. 24).

ENHARMONIC NOTES Two notes that sound the same but are written differently (p. 37).

FERMATA 𝄐 Hold the note for longer than its normal value (p. 30).

FINE The end (p. 31).

1st and 2nd ENDINGS Play or sing through the 1st ending to the repeat sign, then go back to the beginning. When repeating, skip the 1st ending and play the 2nd (p. 22).

FLAT ♭ Lowers the pitch by one half step (p. 34).

FORTE 𝆑 Loud (p. 28).

FORTISSIMO 𝆑𝆑 Very loud (p. 28).

GRAND STAFF The bass staff and treble staff connected by a brace and a line (p. 6).

HALF NOTE ♩ In time signatures with 4 as the bottom number, it receives 2 beats (p. 10).

HALF REST ▬ In time signatures with 4 as the bottom number, it receives 2 beats of silence (p. 13).

HALF STEP The distance from any key on the keyboard to the very next key above or below, whether black or white (p. 37).

LARGO Very slow (p. 29).

LEDGER LINE Short lines which are added to extend the range of the staff when the notes are too low or too high to be written on the staff (p. 6).

LEGATO To play or sing 2 or more notes smoothly connected (p. 19).

MEASURE (or BAR) The area between two bar lines (p. 11).

MEZZO moderately (p. 28).

MEZZO FORTE 𝆐𝆑 Moderately loud (p. 28).

MEZZO PIANO 𝆐𝆏 Moderately soft (p. 28).

MIDDLE C The note in the middle of the grand staff and the C nearest the middle of the keyboard (p. 4).

MODERATO Moderately (p. 29).

NATURAL SIGN ♮ The natural sign before a note cancels a previous flat or sharp (p. 36).

NOTES 𝅝 𝅗𝅥 ♩ ♪ The oval-shaped symbols that are placed on the lines and in the spaces of the staff. They represent musical sounds called pitches (p. 3).

PIANISSIMO 𝆏𝆏 Very soft (p. 28).

PIANO 𝆏 Soft (p. 28).

PITCH A musical sound (p. 3).

QUARTER NOTE ♩ In time signatures with 4 as the bottom number, it receives 1 beat (p. 10).

QUARTER REST 𝄽 In time signatures with 4 as the bottom number, it receives 1 beat of silence (p. 13).

REPEAT SIGN :‖ Return to the beginning or previous repeat sign ‖: at the beginning of the section (p. 22).

RITARDANDO (ritard. or rit.) Gradually slower (p. 29).

SFORZANDO 𝆑𝆰 or 𝆑𝆷 A sudden, strong accent (p. 30).

SHARP ♯ Raises the pitch by one half step (p. 35).

SLUR Smoothly connects two or more notes of different pitches by a curved line over or under the notes (p. 19).

STACCATO ♩• Play the note short and detached (p. 30).

STAFF The five lines and the four spaces between them on which music notes and other symbols are written (p. 3).

TEMPO A word meaning "rate of speed". It tells how fast or slow to play the music (p. 29).

TENUTO ♩ Hold the note for its full value (p. 30).

TIE Two notes of the same pitch joined by a curved line over or under the note. Each note joined by a tie is held for its full value but only the first note is played or sung (p. 19).

TIME SIGNATURE ⁴⁄₄ ³⁄₄ ²⁄₄ Appears at the beginning of the music after the clef sign. It contains two numbers. The upper number tells how many beats are in each measure; the lower number indicates what type of note receives 1 beat (p. 12).

TREBLE (or G) CLEF The clef used for notes in the higher pitch ranges (p. 4).

TREBLE STAFF The staff on which the treble clef is placed. The curl of the clef circles the line on which the note G is placed (p. 4).

VIVACE Lively and fast (p. 29).

WHOLE NOTE 𝅝 In time signatures with 4 as the bottom number, it receives 4 beats (p. 10).

WHOLE REST ▬ Means to rest for a whole measure. In ³⁄₄ it receives 3 beats; in ⁴⁄₄ it receives 4 beats; in ²⁄₄ it receives 2 beats (p. 13).

WHOLE STEP The distance from any key on the keyboard to two keys above or below (p. 37).

Alfred's
Essentials of MUSIC THEORY

LESSONS • EAR TRAINING • WORKBOOK

ANSWER KEY
Book 2
Pages 41–80   Lessons 26–50

TABLE OF CONTENTS
Book 2

Tetrachords and Major Scales

The word TETRA means four. A TETRACHORD is a series of four notes having a pattern of whole step, whole step, half step. The four notes of a tetrachord must be in alphabetical order.

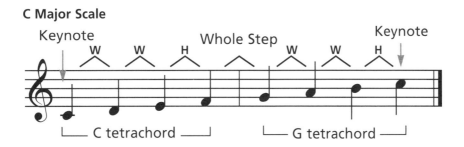

The MAJOR SCALE consists of eight notes—
two tetrachords joined by a whole step.

Each scale begins and ends on a note of
the same name, called the KEYNOTE.
A scale can begin on any note.

The tones of a scale are also called the DEGREES (or steps) of the scale.

There are eight degrees
in a major scale:

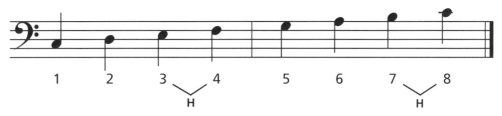

In all major scales, half steps occur between the 3rd and 4th
and the 7th and 8th scale degrees.

The distances between all other scale degrees are whole steps.

Exercises

1 Write tetrachords starting on the following notes, then add the note names under the staff. The notes must be in alphabetical order. Write where the whole (W) and half (H) steps occur above the staff.

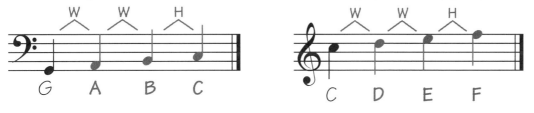

2 Write a C major scale. Add the scale degrees under each note and indicate where the whole and half steps occur above the staff.

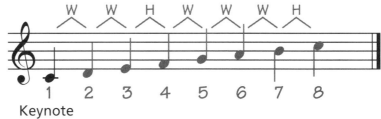

3 Write whether the distance between each note is a whole step (W) or half step (H).

The Sharp Scales — G and D Major

Using the same pattern for tetrachords of whole step, whole step, half step, you can build the sharp scale of G major with the G and D tetrachords. G is the 2nd tetrachord of the C major scale.

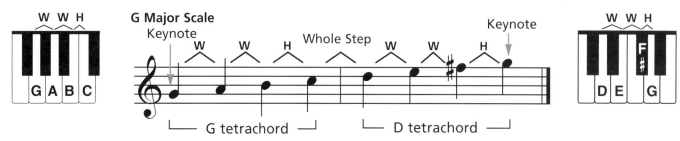

The F must be raised to F♯ to create a whole step.
An F♯ is used instead of G♭ to stay in alphabetical order.

Using the same pattern for tetrachords, you can build the sharp scale of D major with the D and A tetrachords. D is the 2nd tetrachord of the G major scale.

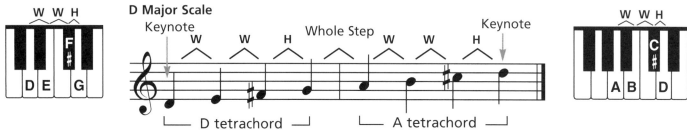

The C must be raised to C♯ to create a whole step.
A C♯ is used instead of D♭ to stay in alphabetical order.

Important!

- The 2nd tetrachord of the C major scale is the 1st tetrachord of the G major scale.
- The 2nd tetrachord of the G major scale is the 1st tetrachord of the D major scale.

  Starting with the C major scale, the 2nd tetrachord is always the 1st tetrachord of the following sharp scale. This overlapping pattern continues through all the major sharp scales.

Exercises

1 Write tetrachords starting on the following notes, then add the note names below the staff. The notes must be in alphabetical order. Remember to include the necessary accidentals. Write where the whole and half steps occur above the staff.

2 Write a G major scale. Add the scale degrees and indicate where the whole and half steps occur.

3 Write a D major scale. Add the scale degrees and indicate where the whole and half steps occur.

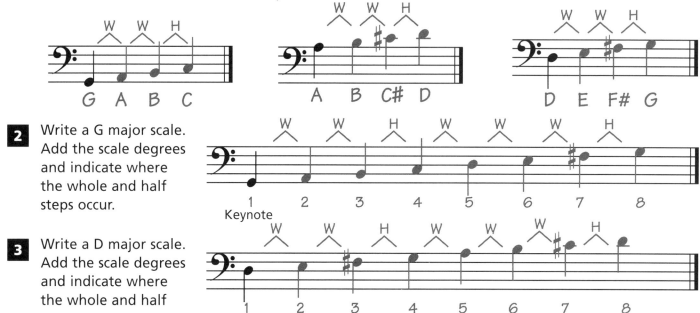

The Flat Scales — F and B♭ Major

Using the same pattern for tetrachords, you can build the flat scale of F major with the F and C tetrachords. C is the 1st tetrachord of the C major scale.

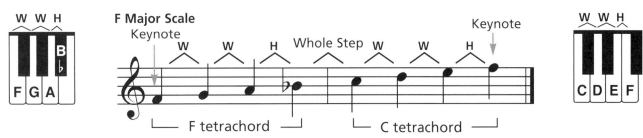

The B must be lowered to B♭ to create a half step.
A B♭ is used instead of A♯ to stay in alphabetical order.

Using the same pattern for tetrachords, you can build the flat scale of B♭ major with the B♭ and F tetrachords. F is the 1st tetrachord of the F major scale.

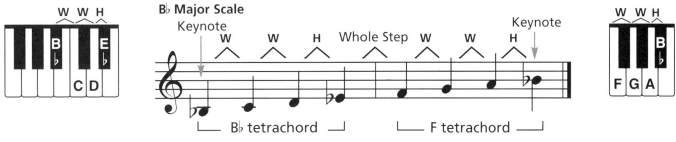

The E must be lowered to E♭ to create a half step.
An E♭ is used instead of D♯ to stay in alphabetical order.

Important!

- The 4th scale degree of the C major scale (F) is the 1st scale degree of the F major scale.
- The 4th scale degree of the F major scale (B♭) is the 1st scale degree of the B♭ major scale.

  Starting with the C major scale, the 4th scale degree is always the 1st scale degree (keynote) of the following flat scale. This pattern continues through all the major flat scales.

Exercises

1 Write tetrachords starting on the following notes, then add the notes names below the staff. The notes must be in alphabetical order. Remember to include the necessary accidentals. Write where the whole and half steps occur above the staff.

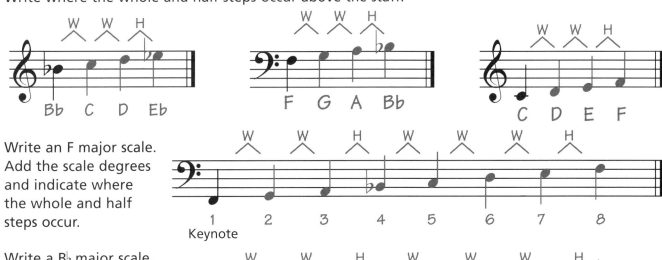

2 Write an F major scale. Add the scale degrees and indicate where the whole and half steps occur.

3 Write a B♭ major scale. Add the scale degrees and indicate where the whole and half steps occur.

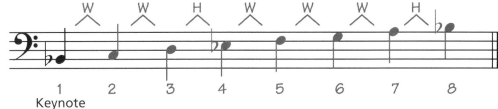

Key Signatures — The Sharp Keys

When writing the scales on page 44, you added sharp signs before the appropriate notes.

In the **G** scale, you added a sharp sign before each F; in the **D** scale, you added sharp signs before each F and C.

To make writing and reading music easier, you can place all of the sharps used in a scale or piece immediately after the clef sign. This is called the KEY SIGNATURE. It indicates the notes that will be sharped each time they appear for the *entire* piece.

In this case, any F will always be played sharp (unless there is a natural sign before the F).

Sharps written in the key signature always appear in a specific order. Here are the sharp key signatures of the scales you know:

Key of G — 1 sharp:
F♯

Key of D — 2 sharps:
F♯, C♯

The order of sharps in the key signature for up to two sharps is **F C.**

Important!

To figure out the name of a major key from the key signature, go up a half step from the last sharp. As an example: a key signature of F♯ would be the key of G major; a key signature of F♯ and C♯ would be the key of D major.

Exercises

1 Write the order of the first two sharps in a key signature.

____F#____ ____C#____

2 If C♯ is the last sharp in the key signature, the major key name would be ____D____.

3 Name the following major key signatures.

a. ____G____   b. ____D____   c. ____D____   d. ____G____

4 Write the following major key signatures.

a. D major   **b.** G major   **c.** G major   **d.** D major

Key Signatures — The Flat Keys

When writing the scales on page 45, you added flat signs before the appropriate notes.

In the **F** scale, you added a flat sign before each B; in the **B♭** scale, you added flat signs before each B and E.

Just like sharp signs, you can place all of the flats used in a scale or piece in the KEY SIGNATURE. It indicates the notes that will be flatted each time they appear for the *entire* piece.

In this case, any B will always be played flat (unless there is a natural sign before the B).

Flats written in the key signature always appear in a specific order. Here are the flat key signatures of the scales you know:

Key of F — 1 flat:
B♭

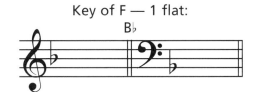

Key of B♭ — 2 flats:
B♭, E♭

> The order of flats in the key signature for up to two flats is **B E.**

Important!
To figure out the name of a major key from the key signature, remember that one flat is the key of F; for two or more flats, the next-to-last flat is the name of the key. As an example, a key signature of B♭ and E♭ would be the key of B♭ major.

Exercises

1 Write the order of the first two flats in a key signature. ___Bb___ ___Eb___

2 If B♭ is the next-to-last flat in the key signature, the major key name would be___Bb___.

3 Name the following major key signatures.

a. ___Bb___   b. ___F___   c. ___F___   d. ___Bb___

4 Write the following major key signatures.

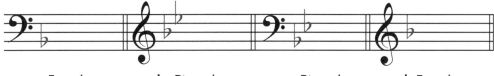

a. F major   b. B♭ major   c. B♭ major   d. F major

UNIT 7 EAR TRAINING FOR LESSONS 26–30

Examples:

1

a.

H

b.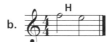

H

c.

W

d.

W

e.

H

f.

W

2

a.

b.

c.

d.

e.

f.

3

a.

b.

c.

d.

e.

f.

Page 48 from the Student Book:

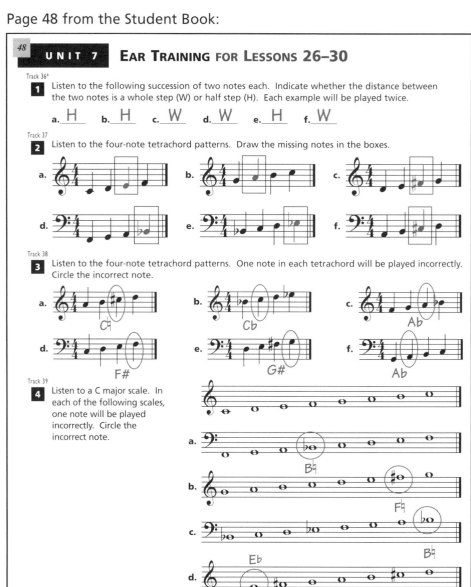

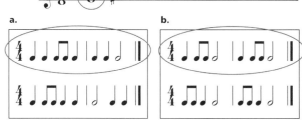

4

a.

b.

c.

d.

5

a.

b.

1 Indicate whether the distance between each note is a whole step (W) or half step (H).

H   W   W   H   W   W   H   H

2 The pattern of a tetrachord is whole step, _whole step_ , _half step_ .

3 Write tetrachords below starting on the following notes. Remember to include the accidentals.

4 Draw a line to match each of the following:

The 2nd tetrachord of: Is the 1st tetrachord of:

D major   D major
G major   G major
C major   A major

5 The major scale is made up of ___2___ tetrachords joined by a _whole step_ .

6 How many notes are in a major scale? _8_

7 In a major scale, half steps occur between the ___3___ & ___4___ and ___7___ & ___8___ scale degrees.

8 Write major scales (without key signatures) beginning on the following notes using whole notes.

a.

b.

9 Fill in the missing notes in the major scales and indicate with an H above the staff where the half steps occur.

a.

b.

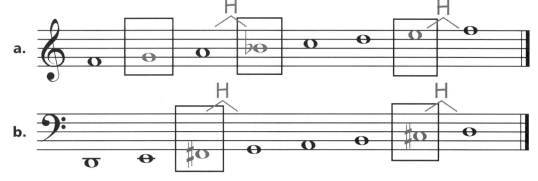

10 Fill in the missing notes and note values in the major scales.

a.

b.

The Remaining Major Scales with Key Signatures

Once you are familiar with how to build tetrachords, it is easy to build any major scale. Altogether, there are 15 major scales: 7 sharp keys, 7 flat keys, and the key of C, which has no sharps or flats.

You are already familiar with the scales and key signatures of five of the 15: C, G (F♯), D (F♯, C♯), F (B♭) and B♭ (B♭, E♭). Here are the remaining 10.

A Major (3 ♯s: F♯, C♯, G♯)

E♭ Major (3 ♭s: B♭, E♭, A♭)

E Major (4 ♯s: F♯, C♯, G♯, D♯)

A♭ Major (4 ♭s: B♭, E♭, A♭, D♭)

B Major (5 ♯s: F♯, C♯, G♯, D♯, A♯)

D♭ Major (5 ♭s: B♭, E♭, A♭, D♭, G♭)

F♯ Major (6 ♯s: F♯, C♯, G♯, D♯, A♯, E♯)

G♭ Major (6 ♭s: B♭, E♭, A♭, D♭, G♭, C♭)

C♯ Major (7 ♯s: F♯, C♯, G♯, D♯, A♯, E♯, B♯)

C♭ Major (7 ♭s: B♭, E♭, A♭, D♭, G♭, C♭, F♭)

The complete order of sharps in the key signature is:
> **F C G D A E B.**

A helpful reminder:
> **F**at **C**ats **G**o **D**own **A**lleys **E**ating **B**read.

The complete order of flats in the key signature is:
> **B E A D G C F.**

A helpful reminder: **BEAD** + **G C F**.

There are, however, only 12 unique *sounding* major scales. The following are ENHARMONIC SCALES; they sound the same but are written differently:

B major sounds the same as **C♭ major**
F♯ major sounds the same as **G♭ major**
C♯ major sounds the same as **D♭ major**

Exercises

1   Name the following major key signatures.

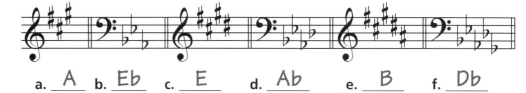

a. ___A___   b. ___E♭___   c. ___E___   d. ___A♭___   e. ___B___   f. ___D♭___

2   Write the following key signatures.

a. E♭ major   b. E major   c. A♭ major   d. C♯ major   e. C♭ major   f. A major

Chromatic Scale

The CHROMATIC SCALE is made up entirely of half steps in consecutive order. On a keyboard, therefore, it uses every key, black and white. When the scale goes up, it is called *ascending*; when the scale goes down, it is called *descending*.

The chromatic scale may begin on any note.
In a chromatic scale, there are 12 tones.

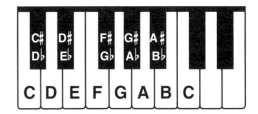

C Chromatic Scale

The ascending chromatic scale starting on C uses sharp signs.

The descending chromatic scale starting on C uses flat signs.

An ascending chromatic scale starting on F looks like this:

A descending chromatic scale starting on G looks like this:

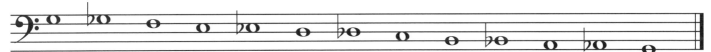

Exercises

1 What is the distance between each pitch in a chromatic scale? _____half_____ _____step_____

2 Write an ascending and descending chromatic scale starting on A.

3 Write an ascending and descending chromatic scale starting on B.

Intervals

An INTERVAL in music is the distance in pitch between two notes. The interval is counted from the lower note to the higher one, with the lower note counted as 1.

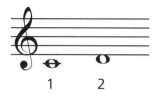

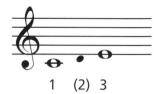

Intervals are named by the number of the upper note (2nds, 3rds, etc.) with two exceptions. The interval between notes that are identical is called a UNISON (also called a PRIME INTERVAL); the interval of an 8th is called an OCTAVE. The intervals below are all written with C as the lower note.

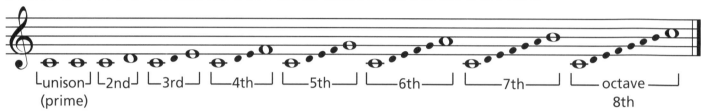

Intervals are called MELODIC INTERVALS when they are sounded separately and HARMONIC INTERVALS when they are sounded together.

EVEN NUMBERED INTERVALS of 2nds, 4ths, 6ths and octaves are written from line to space or space to line.

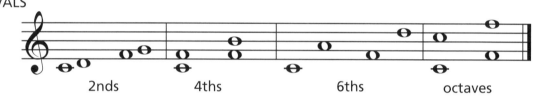

ODD NUMBERED INTERVALS of unisons, 3rds, 5ths and 7ths are written from line to line or space to space.

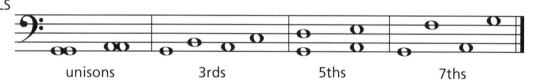

Exercises

1 Name the intervals.

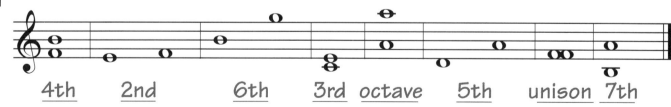

4th   2nd   6th   3rd octave   5th   unison 7th

2 Indicate whether the following are melodic (M) or harmonic (H) intervals.

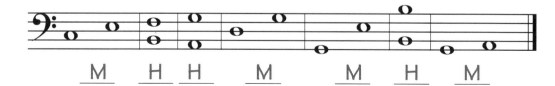

M   H   H   M   M   H   M

3 Write the harmonic interval indicated above the following notes.

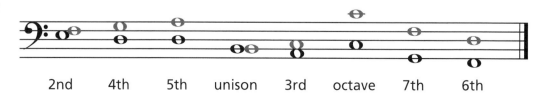

2nd   4th   5th   unison   3rd   octave   7th   6th

Circle of Fifths

The CIRCLE OF FIFTHS is useful in understanding scales and key signatures. It shows the relationship of one key to another by the number of sharps or flats in the key signature and the order in which the sharps or flats occur.

SHARP KEYS
Start with C and go clockwise in *ascending* tetrachord order.

FLAT KEYS
Start with C and go counterclockwise in *descending* tetrachord order.

The sharp keys *ascend* by 5ths (W W H W);* the flat keys *descend* by 5ths (H W W W).

SHARP SCALES
Starting with C, the 2nd tetrachord of the *ascending* major scale becomes the 1st tetrachord of the following ascending scale. The scale's name is derived from the 1st note of that tetrachord, and one sharp is added to the key signature.

FLAT SCALES
Starting with C, the 2nd tetrachord of the *descending* major scale becomes the 1st tetrachord of the following descending scale. The scale's name is derived from the 1st note of that *descending* tetrachord, and one flat is added to the key signature.

OPTIONAL
Another way to determine the order of the flat keys is to ascend by 4ths (W W H). Starting on C: C to F, F to B♭, B♭ to E♭, etc.

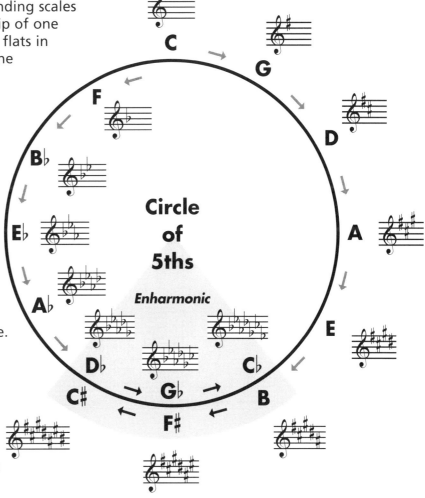

The order of sharps in the key signature:
F C G D A E B.

The order of flats in the key signature:
B E A D G C F.

OVERLAPPING TETRACHORD PATTERNS

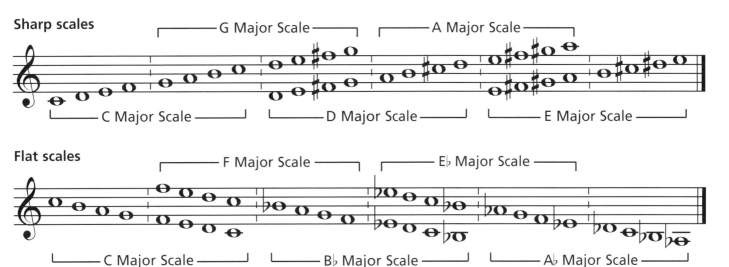

*W=Whole Step. H=Half Step.

UNIT 8 EAR TRAINING FOR LESSONS 31–34

Page 54 from the Student Book:

Examples:

1 Play Examples 1a–1d (right).

2 Play Examples 2a–2d (right).

3 Play Examples 3a–3d (right).

4 Play Example 4 (right).

5

a.

b.

c.

6

7 Play an ascending chromatic scale beginning on middle C, then play the following exercises.

a.

b.

c.

d.

e.

f.

---

54 **UNIT 8 EAR TRAINING FOR LESSONS 31–34**

Track 41
1 For each example you will hear a whole step that moves up or down. Draw the second note on the staff using a half note.

a. b. c. d.

Track 42
2 For each example you will hear a half step that moves up or down. Draw the second note on the staff using a quarter note.

a. b. c. 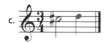 d.

Track 43
3 For each example you will hear a whole step or a half step that moves up or down. Draw the second note on the staff using a quarter note. Each example will be played twice.

a. b. c. d.

Track 44
4 Listen to the melody in the key of F major. Draw the missing notes in the boxes. The example will be played twice.

Track 45
5 Listen to the major scales. One note in each scale will be played incorrectly. Circle the incorrect note.

a.

b.

c.

Track 46
6 Listen to the major scale. Circle the correct rhythm pattern.

a. b.

Track 47
7 Listen to an ascending C chromatic scale. Next, eight ascending notes will be played in the following examples. Write whether it is a major (M) or chromatic (C) scale.

a. _M_ b. _C_ c. _C_ d. _M_ e. _M_ f. _C_

Track 48
8 Listen to a descending C chromatic scale. Next, eight descending notes will be played in the following examples. Write whether it is a major (M) or chromatic (C) scale.

a. _M_ b. _C_ c. _C_ d. _M_ e. _M_ f. _C_

Track 49
9 Listen to the example in the key of D major. Write the missing notes and rhythms in the boxes. The example will be played twice.

8 Play a descending chromatic scale beginning one octave above middle C, then play the following exercises.

a.  d.

b.  e.

c.  f.

9 Play Example 9

1 What is the complete order of sharps in a key signature? __F, C, G, D, A, E, B__

2 Name the following major key signatures.

a. __E__   b. __G__   c. __D__   d. __A__

3 Write the following key signatures.

a. A major   **b.** G major   **c.** E major   **d.** D major

4 What is the complete order of flats in a key signature? __B, E, A, D, G, C, F__

5 Name the following major key signatures.

 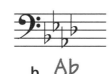  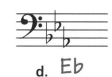

a. __Bb__   b. __Ab__   c. __F__   d. __Eb__

6 Write the following key signatures.

 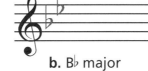  

a. Eb major   **b.** Bb major   **c.** F major   **d.** Ab major

7 The Cb major scale sounds the same as which other major scale? __B__

8 The Gb major scale sounds the same as which other major scale? __F#__

9 The Db major scale sounds the same as which other major scale? __C#__

10 The chromatic scale is made up entirely of __half__ __steps__ in consecutive order.

11 Name the melodic intervals.

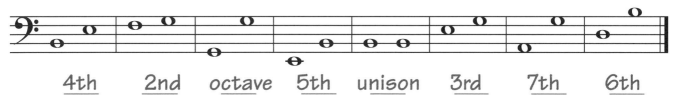

__4th__   __2nd__   __octave__   __5th__   __unison__   __3rd__   __7th__   __6th__

12 Write the indicated harmonic interval above the following notes.

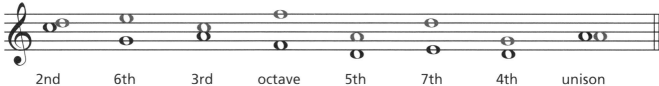

2nd   6th   3rd   octave   5th   7th   4th   unison

13 In the circle of fifths, go clockwise and ascend by 5ths for the __sharp__ keys, and counterclockwise and descend by 5ths for the __flat__ keys.

Perfect and Major Intervals

The interval between the keynote of a major scale and the unison, 4th, 5th or octave of that scale is called a PERFECT INTERVAL.

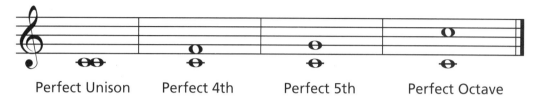

Perfect Unison   Perfect 4th   Perfect 5th   Perfect Octave

The interval between the keynote of a major scale and the 2nd, 3rd, 6th or 7th of that scale is called a MAJOR INTERVAL.

Major 2nd   Major 3rd   Major 6th   Major 7th

THE DIATONIC INTERVALS OF THE MAJOR SCALE

When the keynote and the upper note of an interval are from the same major scale, it is called a DIATONIC INTERVAL. All diatonic intervals in the major scale are either perfect (P) or major (M). The perfect intervals are the unison, 4th, 5th and octave; the major intervals are the 2nd, 3rd, 6th and 7th. This is true for all major scales. P1 indicates a perfect unison; P8 indicates a perfect octave.

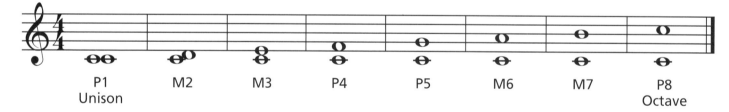

P1   M2   M3   P4   P5   M6   M7   P8
Unison   Octave

Exercises

1 Name the harmonic intervals and indicate whether they are perfect or major.

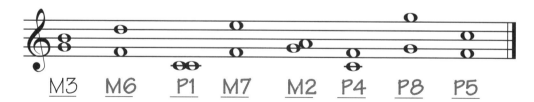

M3   M6   P1   M7   M2   P4   P8   P5

2 Write the note above the given note to complete the harmonic interval.

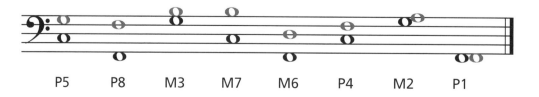

P5   P8   M3   M7   M6   P4   M2   P1

Minor Intervals

When the interval between the two notes of a major interval (2nd, 3rd, 6th or 7th) is decreased by a *half step*, they become MINOR INTERVALS. For example, a major 3rd (M3) becomes a minor 3rd (m3) when decreased by a half step. A small letter "m" is used to signify a minor interval. Only major intervals may be made into minor intervals—perfect intervals may not.

How major intervals may be changed to minor intervals:

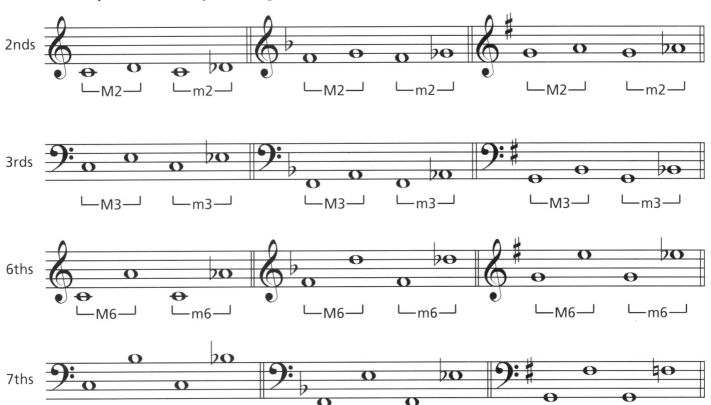

Exercises

1 Name the intervals.

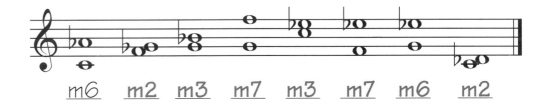

m6 m2 m3 m7 m3 m7 m6 m2

2 Write the note above the given note to complete the harmonic interval.

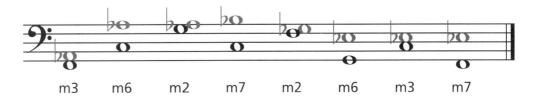

m3 m6 m2 m7 m2 m6 m3 m7

3 Name the intervals, indicating whether they are perfect (P), major (M) or minor (m).

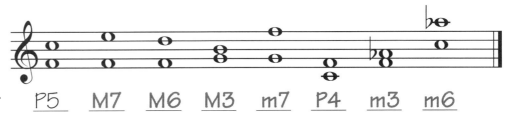

P5 M7 M6 M3 m7 P4 m3 m6

Augmented and Diminished Intervals

The word *augmented* means "made larger." When a perfect or major interval is made larger by a *half step,* it becomes an AUGMENTED INTERVAL. For example, a perfect 5th (P5) becomes an augmented 5th (aug 5). To raise a sharp note by a half step, use a DOUBLE SHARP 𝄪 .

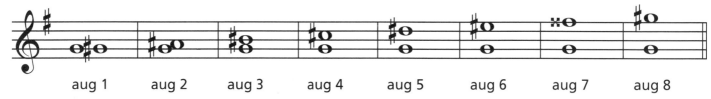

| aug 1 | aug 2 | aug 3 | aug 4 | aug 5 | aug 6 | aug 7 | aug 8 |

The word *diminished* means "made smaller." With the exception of the perfect unison, any perfect or minor interval that is made smaller by a *half step* becomes a DIMINISHED INTERVAL. For example, a perfect 4th (P4) becomes a diminished 4th (dim 4). To lower a flat note by a half step, use a DOUBLE FLAT 𝄫 .

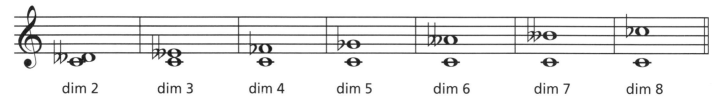

| dim 2 | dim 3 | dim 4 | dim 5 | dim 6 | dim 7 | dim 8 |

Since lowering either note of a perfect unison would actually *increase* its size, the perfect unison cannot be diminished, only augmented.

When the keynote and the upper note of an interval are *not* from the same major scale, it is called a CHROMATIC INTERVAL. Minor, diminished, and augmented intervals are always chromatic intervals in major keys.

Exercises

1 Name the augmented intervals.

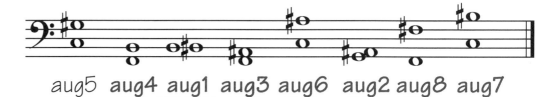

aug5   aug4   aug1   aug3   aug6   aug2   aug8   aug7

2 Write the note above the given note to complete the augmented harmonic interval.

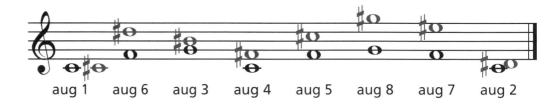

aug 1   aug 6   aug 3   aug 4   aug 5   aug 8   aug 7   aug 2

3 Name the diminished intervals.

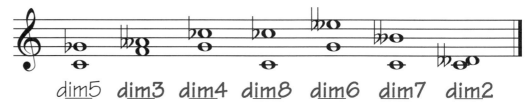

dim5   dim3   dim4   dim8   dim6   dim7   dim2

4 Write the note above the given note to complete the diminished harmonic interval.

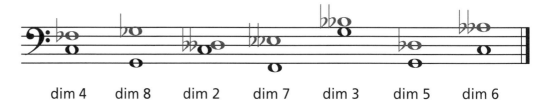

dim 4   dim 8   dim 2   dim 7   dim 3   dim 5   dim 6

Solfège and Transposition

SOLFÈGE is a system of reading notes by assigning a different syllable to each note.
The following syllables are used for all major scales as they relate to the scale degrees:

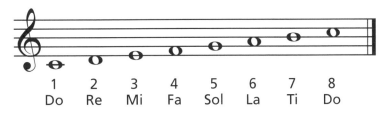

| 1 | 2 | 3 | 4 | 5 | 6 | 7 | 8 |
| Do | Re | Mi | Fa | Sol | La | Ti | Do |

MOVEABLE DO means that the syllables apply to the same scale degrees, regardless of what key you are in. For example, in the key of C, the keynote C is called "Do". In the key of F, the keynote F is also called "Do".

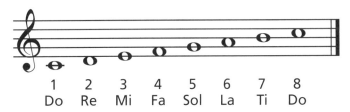

| 1 | 2 | 3 | 4 | 5 | 6 | 7 | 8 |
| Do | Re | Mi | Fa | Sol | La | Ti | Do |

| 1 | 2 | 3 | 4 | 5 | 6 | 7 | 8 |
| Do | Re | Mi | Fa | Sol | La | Ti | Do |

When a melody is rewritten with the exact same sequence of notes and intervals into another key, it is called TRANSPOSITION. This raises or lowers the notes to make a melody easier to sing or play, or so it can be played by an instrument in another key.

The easiest way to transpose is by interval. For example, if a melody is in the key of C and you want to transpose it to the key of D, then you would rewrite all notes a major 2nd higher.

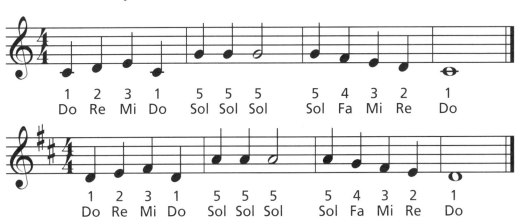

| 1 | 2 | 3 | 1 | 5 | 5 | 5 | 5 | 4 | 3 | 2 | 1 |
| Do | Re | Mi | Do | Sol | Sol | Sol | Sol | Fa | Mi | Re | Do |

| 1 | 2 | 3 | 1 | 5 | 5 | 5 | 5 | 4 | 3 | 2 | 1 |
| Do | Re | Mi | Do | Sol | Sol | Sol | Sol | Fa | Mi | Re | Do |

Exercises

1 Write the syllable names under the notes of the following melody.

Do Mi Sol Do Ti La Fa Re Do

2 Add solfège syllables, then transpose the following melody up a major 2nd adding solfège syllables. Add the new key signature.

Do   La Fa   Sol Fa Mi Re   Do   Do   La Fa   Sol Fa Mi Re   Do

3 Add solfège syllables, then transpose the following melody down a major 2nd adding solfège syllables. Add the new key signature.

Mi   Do   Sol Re Mi   Do   Mi   Do   Sol Re Mi   Do

In the exercises below, you will hear notes *above* or *below* the given notes. For each example, write the note as a melodic half note in the first measure and a harmonic whole note in the second measure. No accidentals are required.

Track 50
1 Major 2nds:

Track 51
2 Major 3rds:

Track 52
3 Perfect 4ths:

Track 53
4 Perfect 5ths:

Track 54
5 Major 6ths:

Track 55
6 Major 7ths:

Track 56
7 Perfect Unison or Octaves:

Track 57
8 Minor 2nds:

Track 58
9 Minor 3rds:

Track 59
10 Minor 6ths:

Track 60
11 Minor 7ths:

1 A perfect interval is the distance between the root of a major scale and the <u>unison</u>, <u>4th</u>, <u>5th</u> or <u>octave</u>.

2 A major interval is the distance between the root of a major scale and the <u>2nd</u>, <u>3rd</u>, <u>6th</u> or <u>7th</u>.

3 The two types of diatonic intervals are <u>perfect</u> and <u>major</u>.

4 Name the intervals below and indicate whether they are major (M), perfect (P) or minor (m).

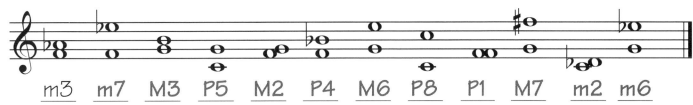

m3　m7　M3　P5　M2　P4　M6　P8　P1　M7　m2　m6

5 Write the notes above the given notes to complete the harmonic interval.

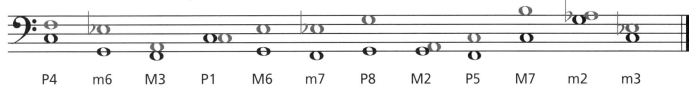

P4　m6　M3　P1　M6　m7　P8　M2　P5　M7　m2　m3

6 A diminished interval occurs when a perfect or minor interval is made: (circle one) **larger** (**smaller**)

7 An augmented interval occurs when a major or perfect interval is made: (circle one) (**larger**) **smaller**

8 Minor, diminished, and augmented intervals are called <u>chromatic</u> intervals.

9 Write the solfège syllable names under the notes of the following melody.

Joy to the World　　　　　　　　　　George Frideric Handel (1685–1759)

Do　Ti　La　Sol　Fa　Mi　Re　Do　Sol　La　La　Ti　Ti　Do

10 Transposition is when a melody is rewritten in another <u>key</u>.

11 Transpose the following melody up a major 2nd and write the new key signature.

Symphony in G, No. 94 ("The Surprise"), 2nd movement　　　　Franz Joseph Haydn (1732–1809)

Sixteenth Notes

Add a flag to the stem of a quarter note ♩ and it becomes an 8th note ♪

Add a flag to the stem of an 8th note ♪ and it becomes a 16th NOTE ♬

In 4/4 time: Two 16th notes equal the duration of one 8th note.

Four 16th notes equal the duration of one quarter note.

In 2/4 , 3/4 and 4/4 time:
a 16th note ♬ is equal to one-quarter count.
For four 16th notes, count "1 e & a" or "ti-ri ti-ri."

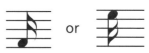

1 e & a 2 (e & a) 3 e & a 4 (e & a)
Ti- ri ti- ri Ta Ti- ri ti- ri Ta

16th notes can be drawn:
• with flags attached to the stems for one 16th note.  or

Write four 16th notes.

• or with 2 beams for two or more 16th notes.

 or 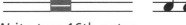  or

Write two 16th notes.   Write four 16th notes.

16th notes can also be combined with 8th notes:

1 (e) & a 2 (e) & a 3 (e) & a 4 (e) & a   1 e & (a) 2 e & (a) 3 e & (a) 4 e & (a)
ti   ti-ri ti   ti-ri ti   ti-ri ti   ti-ri   ti- ri ti   ti-ri ti   ti- ri ti   ti- ri ti

Exercises

1 Add stems with flags or beams to make 16th notes as indicated.

a. Flags   b. Beams (two sets)   c. Flags   d. Beam (one set)

2 Fill in the correct number:

a. __4__ ♬ = ♪

b. __2__ ♬ = ♪

c. __8__ ♬ = 𝅗𝅥

d. __16__ ♬ = 𝅝

3 Write one note equal to the value of the notes preceding it.

a. ♬ + ♪ = _____ ♩

b. ♩ + ♬ = _____ 𝅗𝅥

c. 𝅗𝅥 + ♬ ♬ = _____ 𝅝

d. ♬ ♬ + ♬ = _____ ♩.

Sixteenth Rests

Add another flag to the stem of an 8th rest  and it becomes a 16th REST .

In $\frac{4}{4}$ time: Two 16th rests equal the duration of one eighth rest.

Four 16th rests equal the duration of one quarter rest.

In $\frac{2}{4}$, $\frac{3}{4}$ and $\frac{4}{4}$ time:
a 16th rest is equal
to one-quarter count.

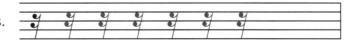

1 e & a 2 e & a 3 e & a 4 e & a

A 16th rest is drawn like this . Write six 16th rests.

Exercises

1   Write the counts under the following example. Clap the rhythm.

1 & 2 e & a 3 & 4 & 1 & a 2 & 3 & 4 & 1 & 2 & 3 e & 4 & 1 e & a 2 e & a 3 & 4 &

2   Fill in the correct number:

a. ___4___ = {   b. ___8___ = ▬   c. ___2___ =   d. ___16___ = ▬

3   Change these 8th notes to
16th notes, then add 16th
rests between them.

4   Write the counts under the notes below the staff.

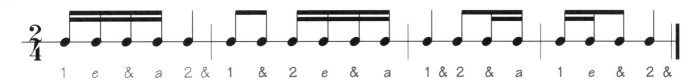

1   e   &   a   2 &   1   &   2   e   &   a   1 & 2   &   a   1   e   &   2 &

5   Complete the measures below with the appropriate rests.
Write the counts under the notes and then clap the rhythm.

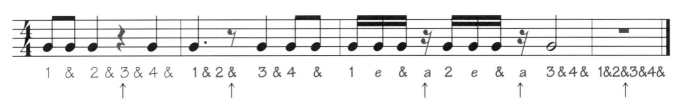

1   &   2 & 3 & 4 &   1 & 2 &   3 & 4   &   1   e   &   a 2   e   &   a   3 & 4 & 1&2&3&4&

Dotted Eighth Notes

Remember: A dot after a note increases its length by one half of its original value.

An 8th note is equal to two 16th notes.

Adding a dot to an 8th note increases its value by half—¼ beat or a 16th note.

A DOTTED 8TH NOTE is equal to three 16th notes.

In $\frac{2}{4}$, $\frac{3}{4}$ and $\frac{4}{4}$ time: a dotted 8th note equals ¾ of a beat.

Here are three ways of writing the same rhythm:

Exercises

1 Write the counts under the following example. Clap the rhythm.

Theme from Farandole   Georges Bizet (1838–1875)

2 Add bar lines to the examples.

a.

b.

3 Complete the measures by adding a note or rest above each arrow.

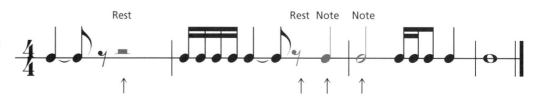

Common Time and Cut Time (Alla Breve)

The time signature $\frac{4}{4}$ may also be written as **C**, called COMMON TIME.

When a vertical line passes through **C**, it is known as CUT TIME **¢** (or ALLA BREVE).
The top and bottom numbers of $\frac{4}{4}$ are cut in half to $\frac{2}{2}$.

In the time signatures of  or $\frac{2}{2}$ **2** means there are 2 beats per measure.
2 means the half note $\half$ receives 1 beat.

In $\frac{2}{2}$ time:

Notes   Rests

$\mathbf{o}$ or $=$ 2 beats $\half$ or $=$ 1 beat $\eighth\eighth$ or $\quarterrest$ = ½ beat

$\half.$ or $=\quarterrest$ = 1½ beats $\quarter$ or $\quarterrest$ = ½ beat $\eighth$ or $\eighthrest$ = ¼ beat

Exercises

1 **C** is known as
__common__ time.

2 **¢** is known as
___cut___ time
or __alla__ __breve__.

3 **¢** has __2__ beats per
measure and the
__half__ note receives
one beat.

*
4 Complete the measures below. Use $\quarter$ or $\half$ notes and $\quarterrest$ or $=$ rests. Clap the rhythm.

1 & 2 &   1 & 2 &   1 & 2 &   1 & 2 &   1 & 2 &   1 & 2 &   1 & 2 &   1 & 2 &

5 In the example below, circle the measures with the incorrect number of beats.

6 In the example below, draw bar lines and a double bar. Count and clap the rhythms.

*Correct student answers may vary.

UNIT 10   EAR TRAINING FOR LESSONS 39–42

Track 61

1 Listen to the 16th notes in the following example.

American Patrol   Frank W. Meacham (1856–1909)

Track 62

2 Listen to a rhythm pattern and write it below. There will be a one measure count-off.
Write the rhythm using the note F. The example will be played twice.

Track 63

3 Listen to the  pattern in the following example.

Trumpet Tune   Jeremiah Clarke (c. 1673–1707)

Track 64

4 Listen to a rhythm pattern and write it below. There will be a one measure count-off.
Write the rhythm using the note D. The example will be played twice.

Track 65

5 Listen to the following example in cut time.

Symphony No. 1 in D Major, 4th movement   Gustav Mahler (1860–1911)

Track 66

6 Listen to a rhythm pattern and write it below. There will be a one measure count-off.
Write the rhythm using the note C. The example will be played twice.

1 Fill in the correct number:

a. __2__ ♪ = ♩   b. __8__ ♪ = 𝅗𝅥   c. __4__ ♪ = ♩   d. __16__ ♪ = 𝅝

2 Add bar lines and a double bar to complete the example below. Clap the rhythm.

Los elefantes   Argentinian Folk Song

3 Fill in the correct number:

a. __16__ 𝄽 = ▬   b. __2__ 𝄾 = 𝄾   c. __4__ 𝄾 = 𝄽   d. __8__ 𝄾 = ▬

4 Complete the measures by adding one rest above each arrow. Clap the rhythm.

5 Add bar lines to complete the example below. Clap the rhythm.

6 Draw the stems and add dots where needed to equal 4 beats per measure.

7 Add bar lines, write the beats under the notes and clap the rhythm.

1 & 2e&a 3 e & 4 &   1e&a 2e&a 3&4&   1 & 2 e & a 3 & 4 &   1e&a 2 & a 3&4&

8 Write one note equal in value to the sum of the notes.

a. ♩ + ♬♬ = ___ 𝅗𝅥   b. ♫ + ♫ + ♩ = ___ 𝅗𝅥.   c. ♬♬ + ♫ + ♩ = ___ 𝅗𝅥.

3/8 and 6/8 *Time Signatures*

In 3/8 time:

3 means there are 3 beats per measure.
8 means the 8th note ♪ receives 1 beat.

In 3/8 time:

♪ or ⌐ = 1 beat

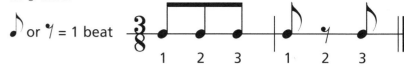

1 2 3 1 2 3

♩ or ⌡ = 2 beats

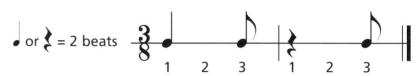

1 2 3 1 2 3

♩. or ▬ = 3 beats

1 2 3 1 2 3

In 6/8 time:

6 means there are 6 beats per measure.
8 means the 8th note ♪ receives 1 beat.

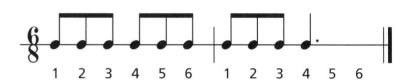

1 2 3 4 5 6 1 2 3 4 5 6

In 6/8 time:

♪ ⌐, ♩ ⌡ and ♩. receive the same number of beats as in 3/8 time.

In addition, ⌡. = 3 beats, ♩. or ▬ = 6 beats

1 2 3 4 5 6 1 2 3 4 5 6

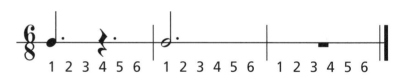

1 2 3 4 5 6 1 2 3 4 5 6 1 2 3 4 5 6

Exercises

1 In the examples, circle the measures with the incorrect number of beats.

a.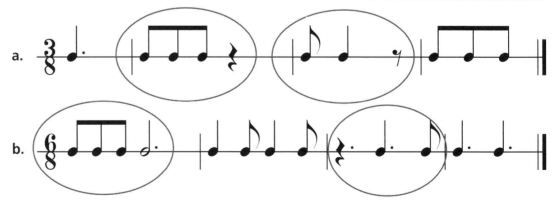

b.

2 Complete the measures, using one note or rest. Write the beats, then count and clap the rhythm.

a.

Note Rest Note Rest

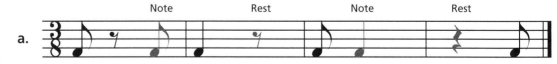

b.

Note Note Note Rest

$\frac{3}{8}$ and $\frac{6}{8}$ *Time Signatures at Fast Tempos*

Remember that $\frac{4}{4}$ or **C** time can be cut in half to **¢** or $\frac{2}{2}$ time when the composer wants the music to be performed at a fast tempo.

$\frac{3}{8}$ and $\frac{6}{8}$ can also be performed at fast tempos: count each $\frac{3}{8}$ measure in 1 count and each $\frac{6}{8}$ measure in 2 counts.

There is a strong beat on 1 in $\frac{3}{8}$ time and on beats 1 and 4 in $\frac{6}{8}$ time. Because the tempo is fast, it is only necessary to count the strong beats.

In fast $\frac{3}{8}$ time:

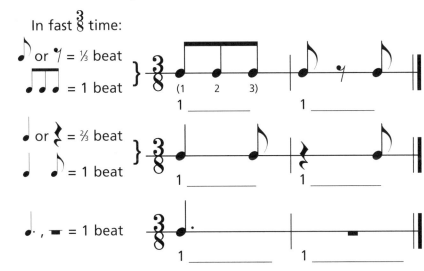

In fast $\frac{6}{8}$ time:

♪ ＇, ♩ ♪ and ♩. receive the same number of beats as in $\frac{3}{8}$ time.

In addition, ♩ = 1 beat, ♩. or ▬ = 2 beats

Exercises

1 Write the strong beats below the notes in a fast tempo.

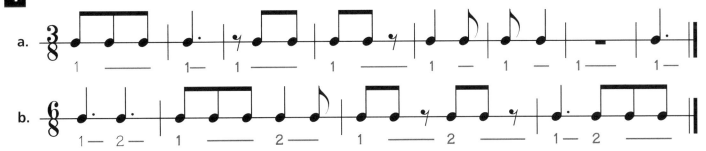

2 Write the correct time signature and the strong beats below the notes in a fast tempo.

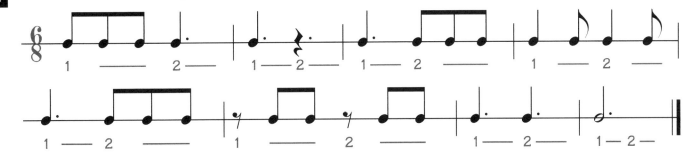

Eighth Note Triplets

When three notes are grouped together with a figure "3" above or below the notes, the group is called a TRIPLET. The 3 notes are played in the time of 2 notes of the same value. It is similar to playing $\frac{3}{8}$ and $\frac{6}{8}$ at fast tempos.

8th NOTE TRIPLETS

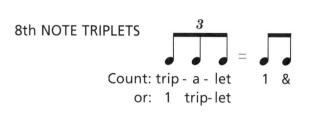

Count: trip - a - let   1 &
or: 1   trip-let

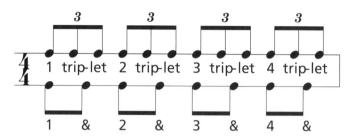

1 trip-let 2 trip-let 3 trip-let 4 trip-let

1 & 2 & 3 & 4 &

March (from the "Nutcracker Suite")   Peter Ilyich Tchaikovsky (1840–1893)

1   &   2 trip - let 3   &   4   &   1   &   2   &   3 & 4 &

Arabesque No. 1   Claude Debussy (1862–1918)

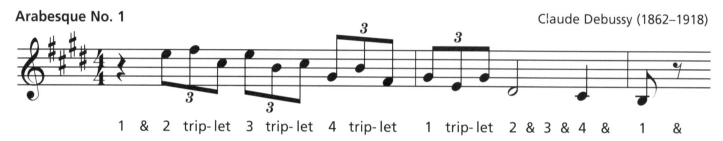

1 & 2 trip- let 3 trip-let 4 trip-let   1 trip-let 2 & 3 & 4 &   1   &

Exercises

1 For each example, add bar lines, write the beats under the notes and clap the rhythm.

a.

1 & 2 &   1   trip - let   2 &   1 & 2 &   1   &   a 2 &

b.

1 & 2 trip-let 3 &   1 & 2 & 3 &   1 & 2 e & a 3 &   1 & 2 & 3 &

2 Complete the incomplete measures below with eighth note triplets. Count and clap the rhythm.

a.

b.

Incomplete Measures (Pick-up Notes)

Some pieces begin with an incomplete measure. This note (or notes) is known as a PICK-UP NOTE.
The following piece has only 1 beat in the first measure. The missing 2 beats are found in the last measure.

Carnival of Venice   Italian Folk Song

Syncopation

When the accent in a musical passage falls on the weak beat (&)
rather than the strong beat (1, 2, etc.), it is called SYNCOPATION.

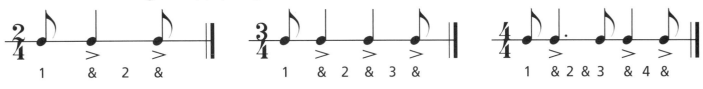

Exercises

1 Fill in the last measure of each example with the correct note value for the given note name.

We Wish You A Merry Christmas   Traditional Carol

Auld Lang Syne   Scottish Folk Song

2 Add bar lines and write the beats under each measure.
Count and clap the rhythm.

UNIT 11 — EAR TRAINING FOR LESSONS 43–46

Track 67

1 Listen to the example. Fill in the missing note and value in the last measure.

Johannes Brahms (1833–1897)

Symphony No. 1

Track 68

2 Listen to the example in a fast $\frac{3}{8}$ time. It is counted in 1 and includes a 2-measure count-off.

We Three Kings of Orient Are

Moderato

Traditional Carol

1 _____ 1 _____ 1 _____ 1 _____ 1 _____ 1 _____ 1 _____ 1 _____

Track 69

3 Listen to the rhythm pattern. Write the missing rhythm in the 3rd measure using the note C. The example will be played twice.

Track 70

4 Listen to the example in a fast $\frac{6}{8}$ time. It is counted in 2 and includes a 1-measure count-off.

For He's a Jolly Good Fellow

Allegro moderato (fast tempo)

English Folk Song

_____ 1 _____ 2 _____ 1 _____ 2 _____ 1 _____ 2 _____ 1 _____ 2 _____ 1 _____ 2 _____ 1 _____ 2 _____

Track 71

5 Listen to the rhythm pattern. Write the missing rhythm in the 3rd measure using the note C. The example will be played twice.

Fast tempo

Track 72

6 Listen to the pattern in the following example. There will be a 3-beat count-off.

Triumphal March (from "Aïda")

Giuseppe Verdi (1813–1901)

Track 73

7 Listen to the rhythm pattern. Write the missing rhythm in the 3rd measure using the note B♭. The example will be played twice.

1   When the first measure is incomplete, the beginning notes are called ___*pick-up*___ notes.

2   Complete the last measure with the correct note value for the given note name.

Star Song   Austrian Folk Song

A

3   When the accent falls on the weak beat, it is called ___*syncopation*___ .

4   Fill in note values to create syncopation and complete the measure.

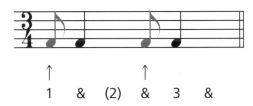

1   &   (2)   &   3   &

5   What type of note receives 1 beat in $\frac{3}{8}$ and $\frac{6}{8}$ time signatures? (Circle one)

6   For $\frac{6}{8}$ time, write the total number of beats.

    a.  = ___2___   b.  = ___5___   c.  = ___3___

7   At fast tempos, $\frac{3}{8}$ is counted in ___1___ , and $\frac{6}{8}$ is counted in ___2___ .

8   At fast tempos, the note that is counted in 1 count in $\frac{3}{8}$ and $\frac{6}{8}$ time is: (circle one)

9   Add bar lines and beats below the notes for the following examples at slow tempos.

Take Me Out to the Ball Game   Albert von Tilzer (1873–1956)

a.

1 2 3   1 2 3   1 2 3   1 2 3   1 2 3   1 2 3   1 2 3   1 2 3

The Flower   Puerto Rican Game Song

b.

5 6   1 2 3 4 5 6   1 2 3 4 5 6   1 2 3 4 5 6   1 2 3 4

10   Three notes grouped together, which are played in the time of two notes of the same value, are called a ___*triplet*___ .

11   Complete the incomplete measures below with 8th note triplets. Add beats below the notes.

1 & 2 & 3 & 4 &   1 & 2 & 3 trip-let 4 &   1 trip-let 2 & 3 & 4 &   1 trip-let 2 & 3 & 4 &

Triads

When three or more notes are sounded together, the combination is called a CHORD. When a 3-note chord consists of a ROOT, a 3rd and a 5th, it is called a TRIAD.

The root is the note from which the triad gets its name.
To build a triad, measure the 3rd and the 5th upward from the root.

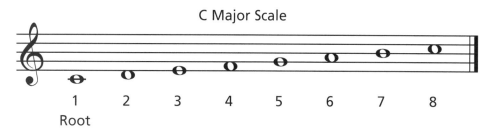

C Major Scale

1   2   3   4   5   6   7   8

Root

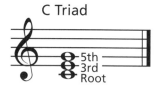

C Triad

The root of a C triad is C. When a triad is in ROOT POSITION, it will include every other note (C-E-G, D-F-A, E-G-B, etc.). *All* the notes will be on lines or *all* the notes will be in spaces.

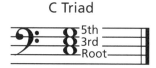

C Triad

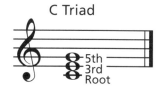

C Triad

Triads may be built on any note of the scale. In the C major scale, the root position triads are:

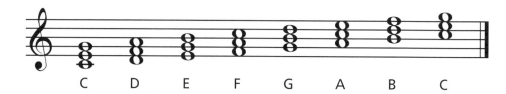

C   D   E   F   G   A   B   C

Exercises

1 Build triads using each of the following *line* notes as the root. Name the root note.

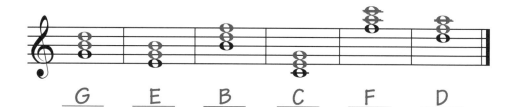

G   E   B   C   F   D

2 Build triads using each of the following *space* notes as the root. Name the root note.

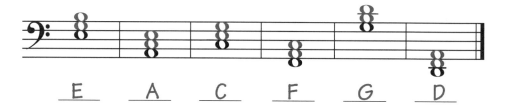

E   A   C   F   G   D

3 Add two notes (above or below) to create a triad in root position from the given 3rd or 5th. Name the root note.

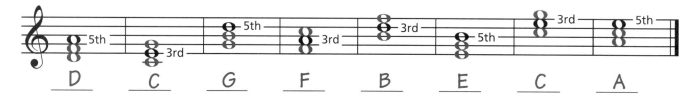

D   C   G   F   B   E   C   A

Primary and Major Triads

The most important triads of a key are built on the 1st, 4th and 5th scale degrees of the major scale. They are called the PRIMARY TRIADS or PRIMARY CHORDS of the key and are identified by the ROMAN NUMERALS **I** (1), **IV** (4) and **V** (5). These three triads contain every tone in the major scale.

The primary triads are MAJOR TRIADS because they consist of the root, a major 3rd and a perfect 5th (see page 56).

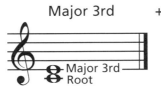 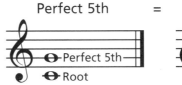 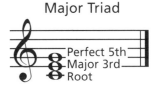

There are two other ways of forming a major triad:

In the key of C major, the
  I   triad (or chord) is the **C** triad (C-E-G).
  IV triad (or chord) is the **F** triad (F-A-C).
  V   triad (or chord) is the **G** triad (G-B-D).

1. select the 1st, 3rd and 5th notes of a major scale.
2. add the interval of a minor 3rd (see page 57) on top of a major 3rd.

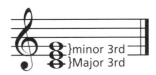

The primary triads in the key of C major:

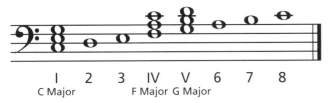

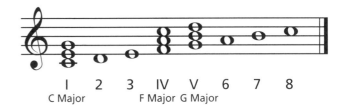

Exercises

1 Build the primary triads in root position for each scale by adding two notes to the 1st, 4th and 5th notes of each scale to complete the triad. Name each triad.

a.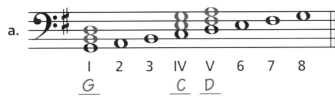

b.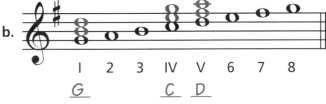

c.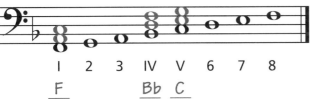

d.

*2 Write the primary triads in root position for each key. Name each triad.

a.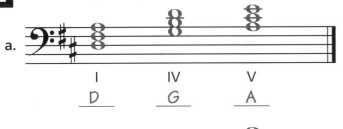

b.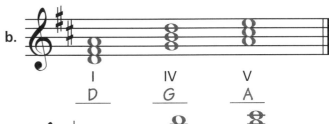

c.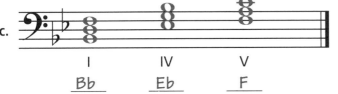

d.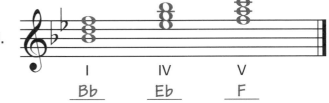

*Correct student answers may vary.

Scale Degree Names

Each tone of a scale can be identified by a name as well as by a **numbered** scale degree (see page 43). The most important scale degrees are the same as those on which the primary chords are built: 1, 4 and 5. The three most important scale degree names are the **Tonic (I), Subdominant (IV)** and **Dominant (V).**

TONIC (I)

The keynote of a scale is called the TONIC. It is the lowest *and* highest tone of the scale. Since the tonic is the **1st** scale degree, it is given the Roman numeral **I**. In C major, C is the tonic note or chord.

DOMINANT (V) and SUBDOMINANT (IV)

The tone a 5th **above** the tonic is called the DOMINANT. Since the dominant is the **5th** scale degree, it is given the Roman numeral **V**. In C major, G is the dominant note or chord.

The tone a 5th **below** the tonic is called the SUBDOMINANT. Since the subdominant is the **4th** scale degree, it is given the Roman numeral **IV**. In C major, F is the subdominant note or chord. The prefix "sub" means under or below.

Important!

The names of scale degrees were derived from an arrangement in which the tonic was the central tone. The subdominant was given its name because it is the same distance **below** the tonic as the dominant is **above** the tonic. It is not called subdominant because it is just below the dominant. See bottom staff.

MEDIANT (iii) and SUBMEDIANT (vi)*

The tone a 3rd degree **above** the tonic (midway between the tonic and the dominant) is called the MEDIANT (a Latin word meaning "in the middle"). Since the mediant is the **3rd** scale degree, it is given the Roman numeral **iii**. In C major, E is the mediant note or chord.

The tone a 3rd degree **below** the tonic (midway between the tonic and the subdominant) is called the SUBMEDIANT. Since the submediant is the **6th** scale degree, it is given the Roman numeral **vi**. In C major, A is the submediant note or chord.

SUPERTONIC (ii) and LEADING TONE (vii)

The tone a 2nd degree **above** the tonic is called the SUPERTONIC. Since the supertonic is the **2nd** scale degree, it is given the Roman numeral **ii**. In C major, D is the supertonic note or chord. The prefix "super" means over or above.

The tone a 2nd degree **below** the tonic is called the LEADING TONE - sometimes called the SUBTONIC. Leading tone is most often used since the note has a strong tendency to "lead" to the tonic, as it does in an ascending scale. Since the leading tone is the **7th** scale degree, it is given the Roman numeral **vii**. In C major, B is the leading tone or chord.

In **scale degree** order, the name and Roman numeral of each scale tone is:

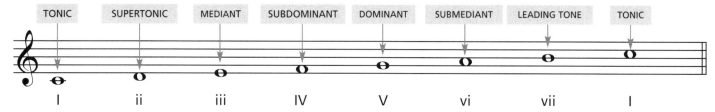

With the tonic being the central tone, the name and Roman numeral of each scale tone is:

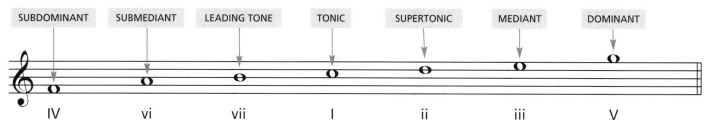

The reason for upper and lower case Roman numerals is explained in Unit 14, Lesson 58.

The V7 (Dominant 7th) Chord

In many pieces, a V7 (dominant 7th) chord is used instead of a V (dominant) triad. To build a V7 chord, add a minor 7th above the root of the V triad (or a minor 3rd above the 5th). The V7 is a chord and not a triad because it has 4 notes rather than 3.

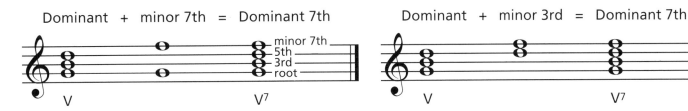

Often, the 5th of the V7 chord is omitted. The V7 chord then would have the same number of tones as the I and IV chords while still retaining the quality of a 7th chord. This also allows the music to be sung or performed by as few as three singers or instrumentalists.

The three primary chords are now I, IV and V7.

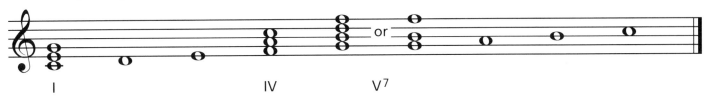

Exercises

* **1** Write the V7 chord for each key. Write the key name and letter name of each chord.

2 Fill in the missing notes in the following V7 chords. Which interval did you add? __5th__

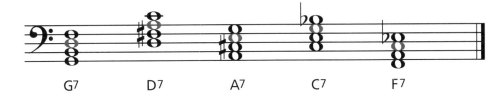

3 Write the following V7 chords with the 5th omitted—include the accidentals.

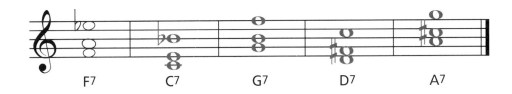

*Correct student answers may vary.

UNIT 12 — EAR TRAINING FOR LESSONS 47–50

Examples:

1

a.

b.

c.

d.

e.

2

a.

b.

c.

d.

e.

Page 78 from the Student Book:

78 UNIT 12 — EAR TRAINING FOR LESSONS 47–50

Track 74

1 Listen to a C major triad. It will first be played one note at a time, and then as a chord (all notes together).

Write whether each example is played one note at a time (1), or as a chord (C).

a. 1 b. C c. C d. 1 e. C

Track 75

2 Listen to the two intervals that make up a major triad: the major 3rd and perfect 5th.

Write whether each example is a major 3rd (M3) or perfect 5th (P5). Each example will be played twice.

Major 3rd + perfect 5th = C major chord

a. M3 b. P5 c. M3 d. P5 e. P5

Track 76

3 Listen to the C major primary triads in root position.

Write whether each chord is a I, IV or V chord. Each example will be played twice.

I IV V I

a. I b. V c. I d. IV e. V

Track 77

4 Listen to the V and the V⁷ chords (with the 5th omitted), played one note at a time and as a chord.

Write whether each chord is a V or V⁷ chord. Each example will be played twice.

V V⁷

a. V b. V⁷ c. V⁷ d. V e. V⁷

Track 78

5 Listen to the three intervals that make up a V⁷ chord: the major 3rd, perfect 5th and minor 7th.

Write whether each example is a major 3rd (M3), perfect 5th (P5) or minor 7th (m7). Each example will be played twice.

Major 3rd + perfect 5th + minor 7th = G⁷ Chord

a. M3 b. m7 c. P5 d. M3 e. m7

3

a.

b.

c.

d.

e.

4

a.

b.

c.

d.

e.

5

a.

b.

c.

d.

e.

1 A chord consists of __3__ or more notes sounded together.

2 A triad consists of a root, a __3rd__ and a __5th__.

3 If the root of a triad is D, the 5th is the note __A__.

4 If the 3rd of a triad is B, the root is the note __G__.

5 Primary triads are built on the following notes of the scale: (circle one)

a. I, II, V   b. I, IV, VI
c. (I, IV, V)   d. II, IV, VI

6 A major 3rd + a __perfect__ __5th__ = a major triad.

7 In a major key, primary triads are always __major__ triads.

8 Another way to form a major triad is by adding the interval of a __minor__ __3rd__ on top of the interval of a __major__ __3rd__.

9 Write the primary triads in the keys of C and G major.

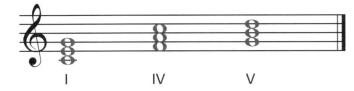

I   IV   V

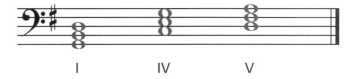

I   IV   V

10 Write the primary triads in the keys of F and D major.

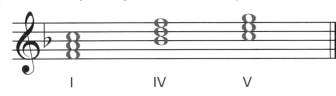

I   IV   V

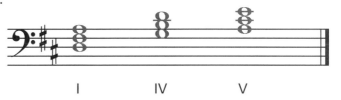

I   IV   V

11 A I chord is also called the __tonic__ chord.

12 A V chord is also called the __dominant__ chord.

13 A IV chord is also called the __subdominant__ chord.

14 A II chord is also called the __supertonic__ chord.

15 A III chord is also called the __mediant__ chord.

16 A VI chord is also called the __submediant__ chord.

17 A VII chord is also called the __leading tone__ chord.

18 Write the following V^7 chords. Include the accidentals.

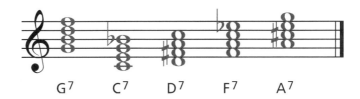

G^7 C^7 D^7 F^7 A^7

GLOSSARY & INDEX OF TERMS & SYMBOLS

Includes all the terms and symbols used in Book 2 and the page on which they are first introduced.

ALLA BREVE see **CUT TIME**. (p. 65).

AUGMENTED INTERVAL When a perfect or major interval is made larger by one half step (p. 58).

CHORD 3 or more notes sounded together (p.74).

CHROMATIC INTERVAL When the keynote and the upper note of an interval are not from the same major scale. Minor, diminished and augmented intervals are always chromatic intervals in major keys (p. 58).

CHROMATIC SCALE

A scale made up entirely of half steps in consecutive order. On the keyboard it uses every key, black or white (p. 51).

CIRCLE OF FIFTHS Shows the relationship of one key to another by the number of sharps or flats in the key signature and the order in which the sharps or flats occur (p. 53).

COMMON TIME 𝄴 Means the same as the time signature of 4/4 (p. 65).

CUT TIME 𝄵 4/4 cut in half to 2/2. It indicates there are two beats per measure and the half note receives 1 beat (p. 65).

DEGREES The tones or steps of a scale. There are eight degrees in a major scale (p. 43).

DIATONIC INTERVAL When the keynote and the upper note of an interval are from the same major scale. All diatonic intervals in the major scale are either perfect or major (p. 56).

DIMINISHED INTERVAL When a perfect or minor interval is made smaller by one half step. (p. 58).

DOMINANT The tone a 5th above the tonic (p. 76).

DOMINANT 7th CHORD A chord built on the 5th scale degree consisting of a root, major 3rd, perfect 5th (sometimes omitted), minor 7th (V7) (p. 77).

DOTTED EIGHTH NOTE ♪. In time signatures with 4 as the bottom number, it receives ¾ of a beat (p. 64).

DOUBLE FLAT ♭♭ Lowers a flat note by a half step (p. 58).

DOUBLE SHARP 𝄪 Raises a sharp note by a half step (p. 58).

EIGHTH NOTE TRIPLET When 3 8th notes are grouped together with a figure "3" above or below the notes (p. 70).

ENHARMONIC KEYS Keys and scales that sound the same but are written differently. The keys of C♯, F♯ and B sound the same as the keys of D♭, G♭ and C♭ respectively (pp. 50 & 53).

EVEN NUMBERED INTERVALS (2nd, 4th, 6th and octave) Written from line to space or space to line (p. 52).

2nd   4th   6th   Octave

HARMONIC INTERVAL Two notes sounded together (p. 52).

INCOMPLETE MEASURE See Pick-up Notes (p. 71).

INTERVAL The distance in pitch between two notes (p. 52).

KEYNOTE The note on which a scale begins and ends (p. 43).

KEY SIGNATURE Indicates the notes that will be sharped or flatted each time they appear. These are placed right after the clef sign (pp. 46 & 47).

LEADING TONE The 7th scale degree (vii) (p. 76).

MAJOR INTERVAL The interval between the keynote of a major scale and the 2nd, 3rd, 6th or 7th of that scale (p. 56).

MAJOR SCALE A scale made up of eight notes—two tetrachords joined by a whole step (p. 43).

Whole Step

C Tetrachord   G Tetrachord

MAJOR TRIAD Triad consisting of a root, major 3rd and perfect 5th (p. 75).

Perfect 5th
Major 3rd
Root

MEDIANT The 3rd scale degree (iii) (p. 76).

MELODIC INTERVAL Two notes sounded separately (p. 52).

MINOR INTERVAL When the interval between the two notes of a major interval (2nd, 3rd, 6th or 7th) is decreased by a half step (p. 57).

MOVEABLE DO In Solfège, Moveable Do means the syllables apply to the same scale degrees, regardless of the key. For example, in the key of C, the keynote C is called "do". In the key of F, the keynote F is also called "do" (p. 59).

OCTAVE The interval of an 8th (p. 52).

ODD NUMBERED INTERVALS (unison, 3rd, 5th and 7th) Written from line to line or space to space (p. 52).

Unison   3rd   5th   7th

PERFECT INTERVAL The interval between the keynote of a major scale and the unison, 4th, 5th or octave of that scale (p. 56).

PICK-UP NOTES Some musical pieces begin with an incomplete measure. This note (or notes) is known as a pick-up note (p. 71).

(1 2) 3

PRIMARY TRIAD/CHORD Triads built on the 1st, 4th or 5th notes of the major scale, identified by the Roman numerals I, IV and V (p. 75).

Perfect 5th
Major 3rd
Root

PRIME INTERVAL See UNISON (p. 52).

ROMAN NUMERALS Numbering system used to identify the scale degree on which the chord is built (p. 75).

ROOT The note from which the chord gets its name (p. 74).

ROOT POSITION A triad where the order of notes from lowest to highest are: root, 3rd, 5th (p. 74).

SIXTEENTH NOTE ♪ In time signatures with 4 as the bottom number, it receives ¼ beat (p. 62).

SIXTEENTH REST 𝄿 In time signatures with 4 as the bottom number, it receives ¼ beat of silence (p. 63).

SOLFÈGE A system of reading musical notes by assigning a different syllable to each note (p. 59).

SUBDOMINANT The 4th scale degree (IV) (p. 76).

SUBMEDIANT The 6th scale degree (vi) (p. 76).

SUPERTONIC The 2nd scale degree (ii) (p. 76).

SYNCOPATION When the accent in a musical passage falls on the weak beat (&) rather than the strong beat (1,2,etc.) (p. 71).

TETRA Four (p. 43).

TETRACHORD A series of four notes having a pattern of whole step, whole step, half step. The four notes of a tetrachord must be in alphabetical order (p. 43).

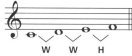

W   W   H

TIME SIGNATURE 𝄴 or 4/4, 𝄵 or 2/2, 3/8 and 6/8 appears at the beginning of a piece of music after the clef sign. It contains two numbers. The upper number tells how many beats are in each measure and the lower number indicates what type of note receives 1 beat (pp. 65, 68, 69).

TONIC The first scale degree or keynote of a scale (I) (p. 76).

TRANSPOSITION When a melody is rewritten with the exact same sequence of notes and intervals into another key (p. 59).

TRIAD A 3-note chord consisting of a root, 3rd and 5th (p. 74).

TRIPLET See 8th note triplet (p. 70).

UNISON The interval between two identical notes (p. 52).

Alfred's
Essentials of MUSIC THEORY

LESSONS • EAR TRAINING • WORKBOOK

ANSWER KEY
Book 3

Pages 81–120   Lessons 51–75

Alfred

TABLE OF CONTENTS
Book 3

Triads — 1st Inversion

Any root position triad may be changed by moving the root (bottom note) of the chord to another position. This is called an INVERSION—it means the notes are rearranged and a tone other than the root is the bottom note of the chord.

The first inversion can be made from a C triad by moving the root (C) to the top of the chord.

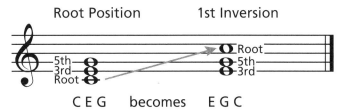

C E G   becomes   E G C

All letter names are the same, but the 3rd (E) is now on the bottom, and the root (C) is now on top. This is called 1st INVERSION.

1st Inversion Triads in C major
(3rd is on the bottom).

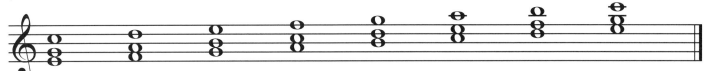

In 1st inversion, the **3rd** is *always* the bottom note.

OPEN and CLOSE POSITIONS

When the notes of a chord are spaced within an octave, it is in CLOSE POSITION.
When the notes of a chord are spaced larger than an octave, it is in OPEN POSITION.

Close Position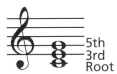

Open Position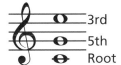

Close Position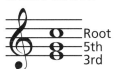

Open Position

Exercises

1 Rewrite the following root position triads in open position.

2 Using the given notes as the root, add the 3rd and 5th *below* each note to make 1st inversion triads in the key of C.

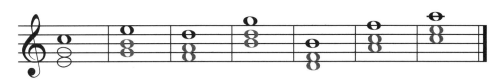

3 Using the given notes as the 3rd, add the 5th and root *above* each note to make 1st inversion triads in the key of C (close position).

Triads — 2nd Inversion

Any 1st inversion triad may be inverted again by moving the lowest note (3rd) to the top.

The second inversion can be made from a 1st inversion C triad by moving the 3rd (E) to the top of the chord.

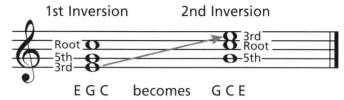

E G C   becomes   G C E

All letter names are the same, but the 5th (G) is now on the bottom, and the root (C) is now in the middle. This is called 2nd INVERSION.

2nd Inversion Triads in C Major
(5th is on the bottom).

In 2nd inversion, the **5th** is *always* the bottom note.

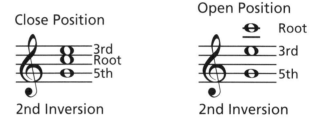

Triads in all Positions (close).

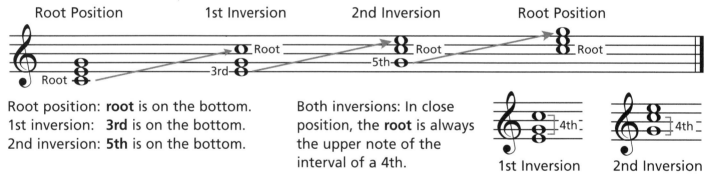

Root position: **root** is on the bottom.
1st inversion: **3rd** is on the bottom.
2nd inversion: **5th** is on the bottom.

Both inversions: In close position, the **root** is always the upper note of the interval of a 4th.

Exercises

1 Rewrite the following close position 2nd inversion triads in open position.

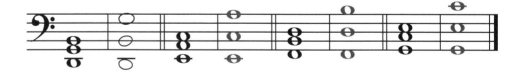

2 Rewrite the following root position triads in 2nd inversion (close position).

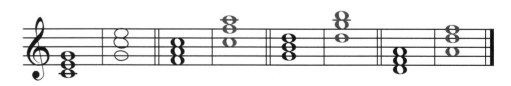

3 Using the given notes as the root, add the 5th *below* and the 3rd *above* to make 2nd inversion triads in the key of C.

V7 Chord—1st, 2nd and 3rd Inversions

The V7 chord can also be inverted. Since the V7 chord is a 4-note chord, it can be written in four different positions: root, 1st inversion, 2nd inversion and 3rd inversion (7th at the bottom).

Close Position

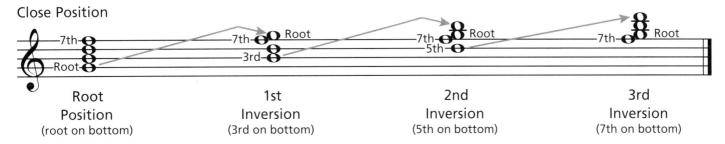

| Root Position (root on bottom) | 1st Inversion (3rd on bottom) | 2nd Inversion (5th on bottom) | 3rd Inversion (7th on bottom) |

In 1st, 2nd and 3rd inversions in close position, the **root** is always the upper note of the interval of a 2nd.

Exercises

1 Write the 1st, 2nd and 3rd inversions for the following V7 chords in close position.

a.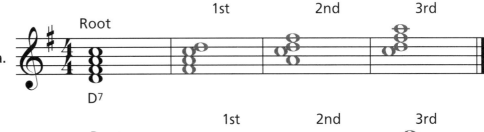

b.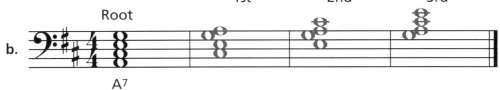

c.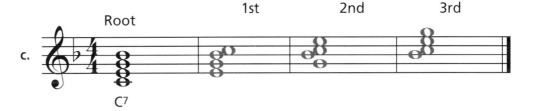

d.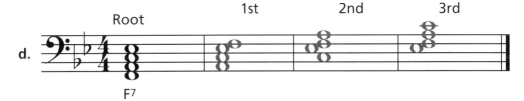

2 Indicate the inversion of the following V7 chords.

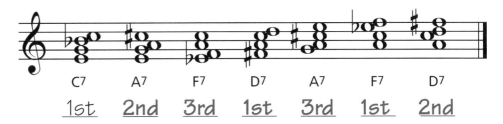

C7 — 1st
A7 — 2nd
F7 — 3rd
D7 — 1st
A7 — 3rd
F7 — 1st
D7 — 2nd

3 Write the following V7 chords in the given inversions. The bottom note is given. Add accidentals where needed

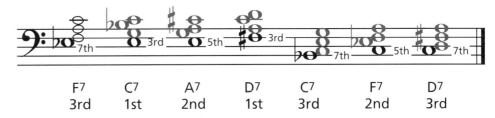

F7 — 3rd
C7 — 1st
A7 — 2nd
D7 — 1st
C7 — 3rd
F7 — 2nd
D7 — 3rd

Figured Bass

To indicate what inversion of a chord to use, numbers are added to the Roman numeral of that chord. This system originated during the BAROQUE PERIOD (1600–1750) and is called FIGURED BASS.

1st Inversion Triads
(3rd is the lowest note)

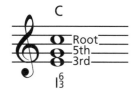

In the key of C, the 1st inversion of the I chord was originally written I_3^6.

The numbers $^6_3$ indicate the intervals of the chord from the bass (lowest) note. The middle note G is up a 3rd from the bass note E, and the top note C is up a 6th. Over time, the bottom 3 was dropped and shortened to I^6.

Another way to indicate a 1st inversion C chord is by using the chord symbol C followed by the bass note, written C/E.

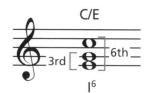

2nd Inversion Triads
(5th is the lowest note)

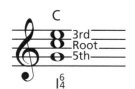

In the key of C, the 2nd inversion of the I chord is written I_4^6. The middle note C is up a 4th from the bass note G, and the top note E is up a 6th.

Another way to indicate a 2nd inversion C chord is C/G.

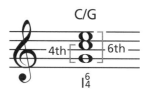

V^7 Chords
The V^7 chord has four different positions.

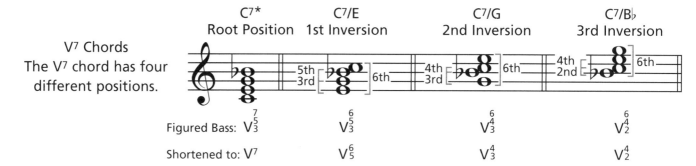

	C7* Root Position	C7/E 1st Inversion	C7/G 2nd Inversion	C7/B♭ 3rd Inversion
Figured Bass:	$V^7_{5\,3}$	$V^6_{5\,3}$	$V^6_{4\,3}$	$V^6_{4\,2}$
Shortened to:	V^7	V^6_5	V^4_3	V^4_2

Letter name chord symbols (C/G) are usually written above the staff.
Roman numeral chord symbols (V^7) are usually written below the staff.

*The C7 chord is the V^7 chord in the key of F.

Exercises

1 Write the chord symbol above the staff and the Roman numeral below the staff, using figured bass where applicable, for each chord in the key of C.

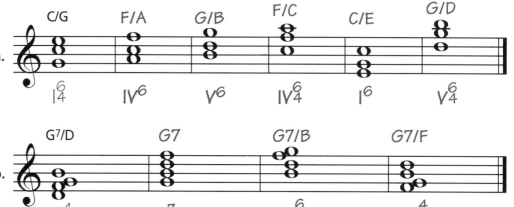

Major Chord Progressions

Chords that move (or progress) from one to another are called a CHORD PROGRESSION. Because the I, IV and V chords contain all the notes of the major scale, they can be used to ACCOMPANY (play along with) most simple melodies. In many chord progressions, a V7 chord is used in place of the V chord.

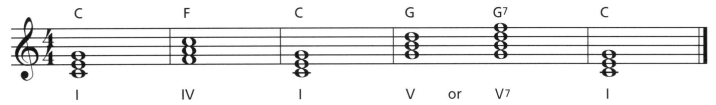

When the IV and V (or V7) chords are in root position, the progression sounds choppy. To make it easier to play and sound smoother, the IV chord often is moved to the 2nd inversion, and the V (or V7) chord often is moved to the 1st inversion.

In the IV chord, the 5th (C) is moved down an octave.

In the V chord, the 3rd (B) and 5th (D) are moved down an octave.

In the V7 chord, the 3rd (B), 5th (D) and 7th (F) are moved down an octave.

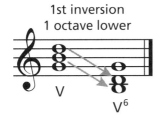

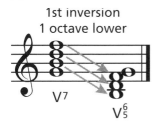

The following positions are often used for smooth progressions. Notice there is a common tone between each chord.

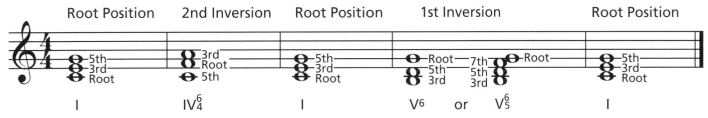

Exercises

*1. Write the chords in root position in the key of G major. Write the chord symbol for each above the staff.

2. Rewrite the above chord progression to make it sound smoother. Add chord symbols.

3. Write the chords in root position in the key of F major. Write the chord symbol for each above the staff.

4. Rewrite the above chord progression to make it sound smoother. Add chord symbols.

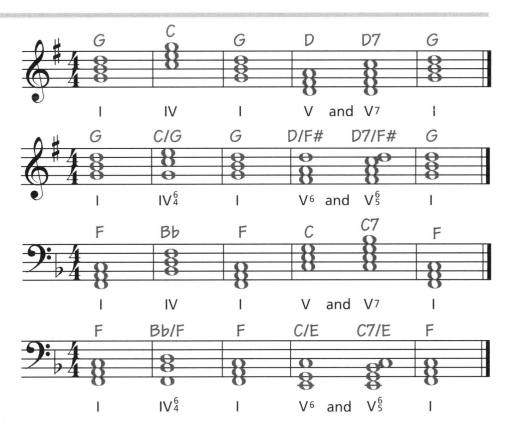

*Correct student answers may vary.

Examples:

1

a. R

b. 1st

c. 1st

d. R

e. 1st

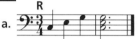

2

a. R

b. 2nd

c. R

d. 2nd

e. 2nd

3

a. 3rd

b. R

c. R

d. 3rd

e. 3rd

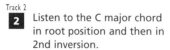

Page 88 from the Student Book:

88 **UNIT 13** **EAR TRAINING FOR LESSONS 51–55**

Track 1*
1 Listen to the C major chord in root position and then in 1st inversion.

Write whether the chord in each example is in root position (R) or 1st inversion (1st). Each example will be played twice.

a. ___R___ b. ___1st___ c. ___1st___ d. ___R___ e. ___1st___

Track 2
2 Listen to the C major chord in root position and then in 2nd inversion.

Write whether the chord in each example is in root position (R) or 2nd inversion (2nd). Each example will be played twice.

a. ___R___ b. ___2nd___ c. ___R___ d. ___2nd___ e. ___2nd___

Track 3
3 Listen to the V⁷ chord in root, 1st, 2nd and 3rd inversions.

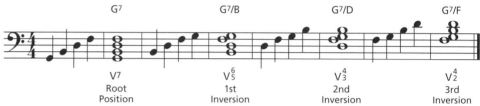

Write whether the V⁷ chord in each example is in root position (R) or 3rd inversion (3rd). Each example will be played twice.

a. ___3rd___ b. ___R___ c. ___R___ d. ___3rd___ e. ___3rd___

Track 4
4 Listen to the chord progression in C major with all chords in root position.

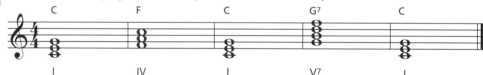

Track 5
5 Listen to the same chord progression with inversions.

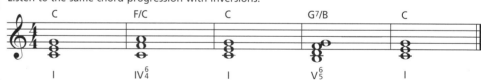

Track 6
6 You will hear I, IV and V⁷ root position chords in the key of C major. Write the Roman numerals for the missing chords on the lines. Each example will be played twice.

a. ___I___ ___IV___ ___I___ ___V7___ ___I___

b. ___I___ ___V7___ ___I___ ___IV___ ___V___

*Track 1 refers to the track number on Ear Training CD 2.

4 Play Example 4, above.

5 Play Example 5, above.

6

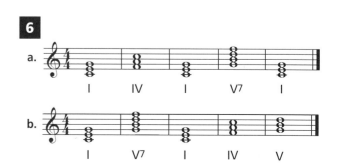

1 An inversion of a chord means the root is no longer on the <u>bottom</u>.

2 In 1st inversion, the 3rd of a triad is always on the <u>bottom</u>.

3 In close position, the notes of the chord are spaced <u>within</u> an octave.

4 Rewrite the following triads in 1st inversion.
Add the chord symbol and the Roman numeral for each chord.

5 In 2nd inversion, the 5th of a triad is always on the <u>bottom</u>.

6 In open position, the notes of the chord are spaced <u>larger</u> than an octave.

7 Rewrite the following root position triads in 2nd inversion.
Add the chord symbol and the Roman numeral for each chord.

8 If the root is on the bottom of a triad, it is in <u>root position</u>; if the 3rd is on the bottom, it is in <u>1st</u> inversion; if the 5th is on the bottom, it is in <u>2nd</u> inversion.

9 In close position, the root in 1st and 2nd inversions is the upper note of the interval of a <u>4th</u>.

10 How many inversions are there of the V^7 chord? <u>3</u>.

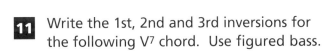

11 Write the 1st, 2nd and 3rd inversions for the following V^7 chord. Use figured bass.

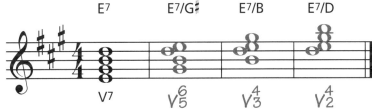

12 Chords that move from one to another, are called a <u>chord progression</u>.

13 The three chords that contain all the notes of the major scale are the <u>I</u>, <u>IV</u> and <u>V</u> chords.

14 On the lower staff, rewrite the following chord progression using inversions so there is a common tone between each chord. Indicate what position each chord is in, using chord symbols and figured bass. Add the chord symbol and the Roman numeral for each chord.

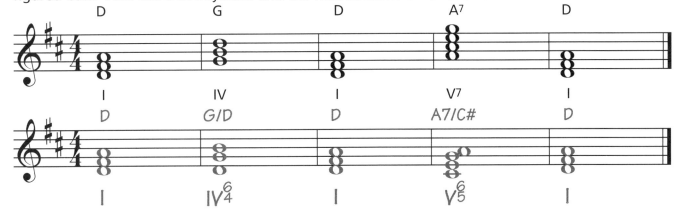

Minor Scales

Remember, there are 15 major scales with unique key signatures—see Book 2, page 50.
For every major key, there is a RELATIVE MINOR KEY that has the *same* key signature.

Each relative minor scale begins on the 6th note of the RELATIVE MAJOR SCALE.
The 6th note is the keynote of the minor scale and the note from which the scale gets its name.

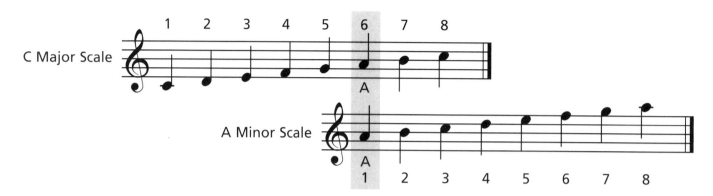

The keynote of a relative minor scale may also be found by *descending* a minor 3rd from the keynote of the major scale.

Conversely, the keynote of the relative major scale may be found by *ascending* a minor 3rd from the keynote of the minor scale.

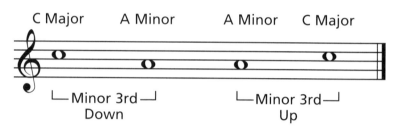

The keys of C major and A minor are relatives because they have the same key signature (no ♯s, no ♭s).

Exercises

1 Write the relative minor key name and the key signature for each major key.

G major: ___E___ minor

D major: ___B___ minor

A major: ___F#___ minor

E major: ___C#___ minor

F major: ___D___ minor

B♭ major: ___G___ minor

E♭ major: ___C___ minor

A♭ major: ___F___ minor

*2 Write the following minor key signatures and scales.

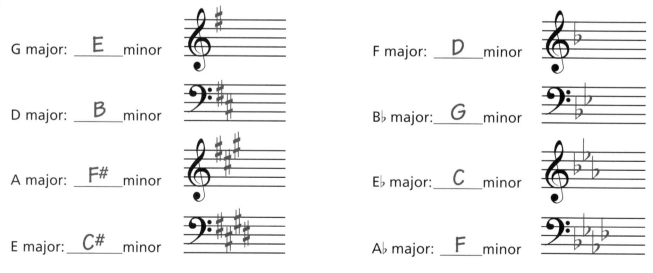

E minor

D minor

*Correct student answers may vary.

Natural, Harmonic and Melodic Minor Scales

There are three types of minor scales: the NATURAL, HARMONIC and MELODIC.

The NATURAL MINOR SCALE uses *only* the tones of the relative major scale.

The HARMONIC MINOR SCALE raises the 7th tone (G)
by a half step *ascending* and *descending*.

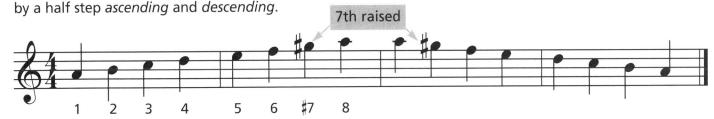

The MELODIC MINOR SCALE raises the 6th (F) and 7th (G) tones by a half step *ascending*.
It *descends* like the natural minor scale.

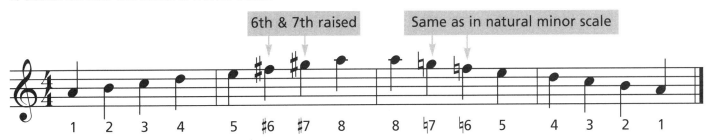

The Harmonic Minor Scale is the most frequently used of the three minor scales.

THE DIATONIC INTERVALS OF THE HARMONIC MINOR SCALE
All diatonic intervals in the harmonic minor scale are either perfect (P), major (M) or minor (m).
The perfect intervals are the unison, 4th, 5th and octave; the major intervals are the 2nd and 7th;
the minor intervals are the 3rd and 6th. This is true for all harmonic minor scales. Compare with the
major scale intervals in Book 2, page 56.

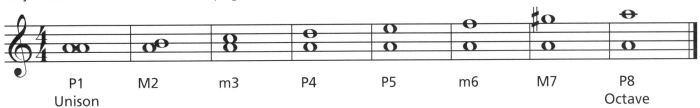

Exercises

1 Write the following harmonic minor scales with key signatures using quarter notes.

E Harmonic Minor

D Harmonic Minor

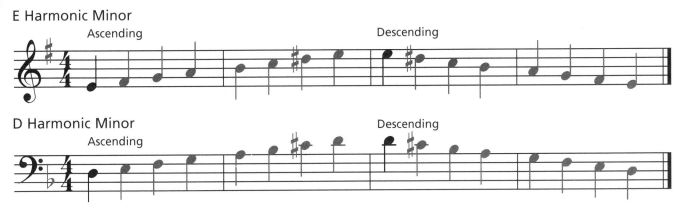

Minor Triads

Just as a major triad can be built from the 1st, 3rd and 5th scale degrees of a major scale,
a MINOR TRIAD can be built from the 1st, 3rd and 5th scale degrees of a minor scale.

Major triads consist
of a root, major 3rd
and a perfect 5th.

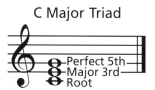

Minor triads consist
of a root, minor 3rd
and a perfect 5th.

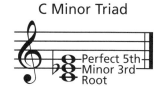

Build a major triad
by adding a minor 3rd
on top of a major 3rd.

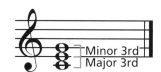

Build a minor triad
by adding a major 3rd
on top of a minor 3rd.

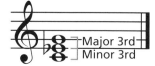

Any major triad may be
changed to a minor triad by
lowering the 3rd by ½ step.

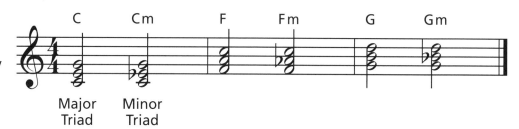

MAJOR and MINOR TRIADS IN THE MAJOR SCALE

In a major scale, only triads with the root on the 1st, 4th and 5th scale degrees are *major triads*.
Triads with the root on the 2nd, 3rd and 6th scale degrees are *minor triads*.

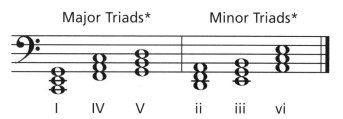

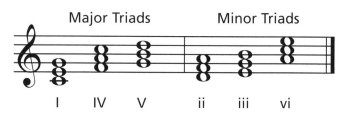

*Major triads are numbered with upper case Roman numerals (I), minor triads with lower case Roman numerals (ii).

Exercises

1 Build minor triads (adding accidentals where necessary) using each of the following notes
as the root. Name the triad.

2 Label each triad in the
keys of F and G major
using upper and lower
case Roman numerals.

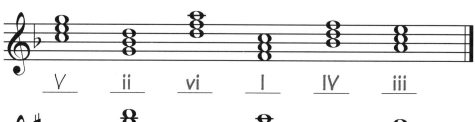

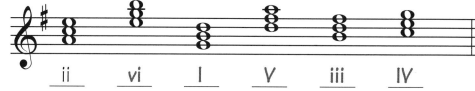

Augmented and Diminished Triads

Major and minor triads can each be altered. Major triads may be made *larger* (augmented) and minor triads may be made *smaller* (diminished).

An AUGMENTED TRIAD is a major triad that has been made larger by *raising* the 5th by ½ step.

A DIMINISHED TRIAD is a minor triad that has been made smaller by *lowering* the 5th by ½ step.

Major Triad  Aug. Triad 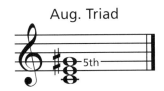 Minor Triad  Dim. Triad

Build an augmented triad by adding a major 3rd on top of a major 3rd.

Aug. Triad

Build a diminished triad by adding a minor 3rd on top of a minor 3rd.

Dim. Triad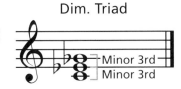

SUMMARY OF MAJOR, MINOR, AUGMENTED AND DIMINISHED TRIADS

Major = major 3rd + minor 3rd
Minor = minor 3rd + major 3rd
Augmented = both 3rds are major
Diminished = both 3rds are minor

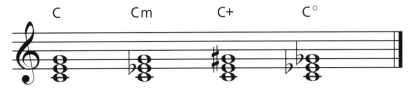

Triads and chords may be indicated by letters and symbols:
Chord letter only = major, m = minor, + = augmented, ° = diminished

MAJOR TRIAD SCALE
In the major scale, triads built on the:
- 1st, 4th, and 5th scale degrees are major triads,
- 2nd, 3rd and 6th scale degrees are minor triads,
- 7th scale degree is a diminished triad.

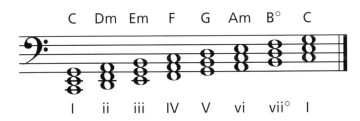 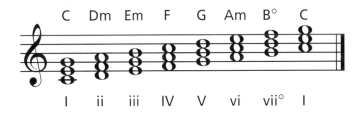

Exercises

1 Write the name of each triad and indicate whether it is major (chord letter), minor (m), augmented (+) or diminished (°).

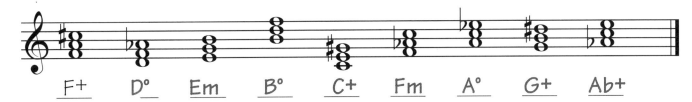

F+ D° Em B° C+ Fm A° G+ Ab+

Examples:

1

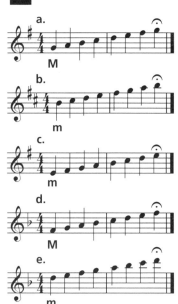

2 Play scales from Example 2, right.

3

4

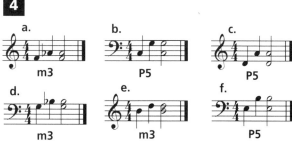

Page 94 of Student Book:

94 **UNIT 14** **EAR TRAINING FOR LESSONS 56–59**

5
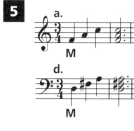
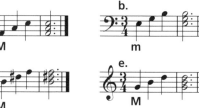

6

7

1 Write the relative harmonic minor scale (adding accidentals where necessary) for each major scale using whole notes.

G Major _____E_____ Harmonic Minor

a.

F Major _____D_____ Harmonic Minor

b.

D Major _____B_____ Harmonic Minor

c.

2 Indicate the relative major scale for each minor scale.
A minor: ___C___ major   E minor: ___G___ major   D minor: ___F___ major

3 The Harmonic Minor Scale: (circle one) (raises) / lowers
the 7th tone by one (circle one) (half) / whole step *ascending* and *descending.*

4 When *ascending,* the Melodic Minor Scale (circle one) (raises) / lowers
the 6th and 7th tones by one (circle one) (half) / whole step.

5 The Melodic Minor Scale *descends* the same as the _____natural_____ minor scale.

6 A major triad consists of a root, ___major___ ___3rd___ and ___perfect___ ___5th___.
A major triad may also be built by adding a ___minor___ ___3rd___ on top of a ___major___ ___3rd___.

7 A minor triad consists of a root, ___minor___ ___3rd___ and ___perfect___ ___5th___.
A minor triad may also be built by adding a ___major___ ___3rd___ on top of a ___minor___ ___3rd___.

8 An augmented triad is a major triad with the ___5th___ raised a half step.
An augmented triad may also be built by adding a ___major___ ___3rd___ on top of a ___major___ ___3rd___.

9 A diminished triad is a minor triad with the ___5th___ lowered a half step.
A diminished triad may also be built by adding a ___minor___ ___3rd___ on top of a ___minor___ ___3rd___.

10 Label each triad major (chord symbol), minor (m), augmented (+) or diminished (○).

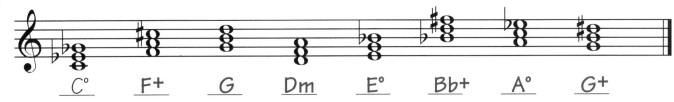

___C°___   ___F+___   ___G___   ___Dm___   ___E°___   ___Bb+___   ___A°___   ___G+___

The Primary Triads in Minor Keys

As in the major keys (see Book 2, page 75), the most important triads of a minor key are built on the 1st, 4th and 5th scale degrees of the minor scale. They are called the PRIMARY TRIADS or primary chords of the key and are identified by the Roman numerals i, iv and V. These three triads contain every note of the minor scale.

A Harmonic Minor

| i | 2 | 3 | iv | V | 6 | 7 | 8 |
| A minor | | | D minor | E Major | | (raised) | |

- Notice that the i and iv chords are minor chords because they consist of the root, a minor 3rd and a perfect 5th (see page 92).

- The V chord is a major triad, as in the major scale, because it consists of a root, major 3rd and perfect 5th. The G is sharped because the A harmonic minor scale has the 7th raised a half step.

HARMONIC MINOR TRIAD SCALE
In the harmonic minor scale, triads built on the:

- 1st and 4th scale degrees are minor triads,

- 5th and 6th scale degrees are major triads,

- 2nd and 7th scale degrees are diminished triads (see page 93),

- 3rd scale degree is an augmented triad (see page 93).

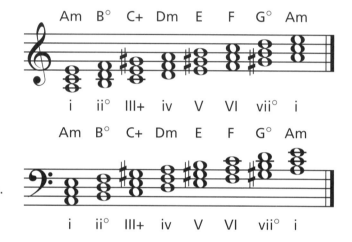

Exercises

1 Build the primary triads for each minor scale by adding two notes to the 1st, 4th, and 5th notes of each scale to complete the triad. Use the harmonic minor scale (raised 7th). Name each triad.

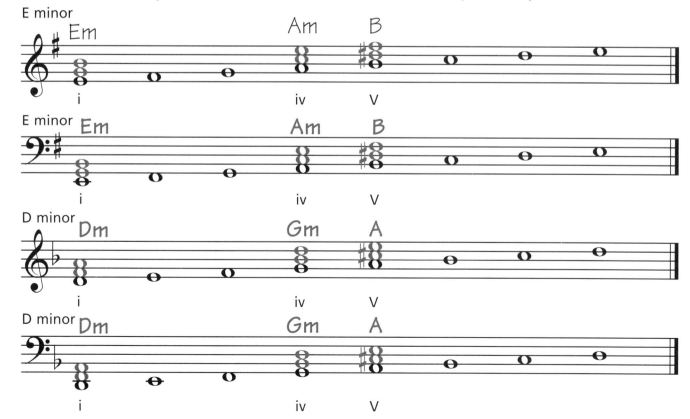

Minor Chord Progressions

Because the i, iv and V triads contain all the notes of the harmonic minor scale, they can be used to accompany most simple melodies in minor keys. In many chord progressions, the V7 chord is used instead of the V triad.

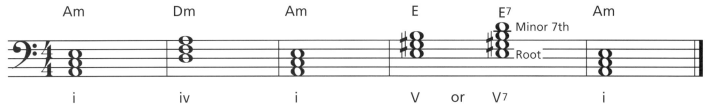

To make this minor chord progression sound smoother, the iv chord is moved to the 2nd inversion, and the V (or V7) chord is moved to the 1st inversion.

In the iv chord, the 5th (A) is moved down an octave.

In the V chord, the 3rd (G♯) and 5th (B) are moved down an octave.

In the V7 chord, the 3rd (G♯), 5th (E) and 7th (D) are moved down an octave.

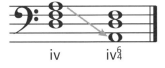
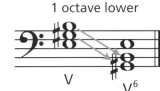

The following positions are often used for smooth progressions. Notice there is a common tone between each chord.

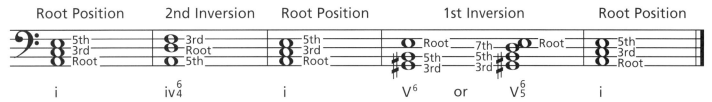

Remember, when a triad is not in root position (close position), the root is always the upper note of the interval of a 4th. When a V7 chord is not in root position (close position), the root is always the upper note of the interval of a 2nd.

Exercises

1 Write the chords in root position in the key of E minor. Write the chord symbols for each above the staff.

2 Rewrite the above chord progression to make it sound smoother. Add chord symbols.

3 Write the chords in root position in the key of D minor. Write the chord symbols for each above the staff.

4 Rewrite the above chord progression to make it sound smoother. Add chord symbols.

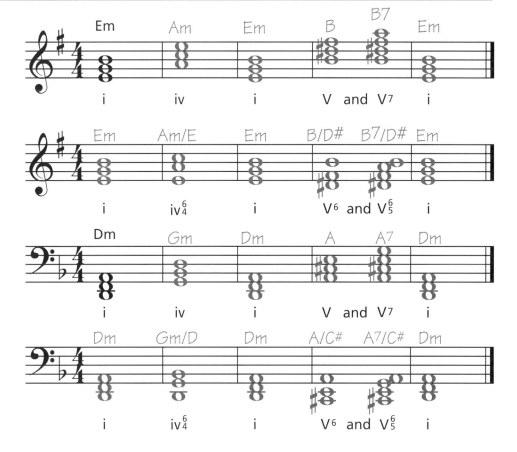

Modes Related to the Major Scale: Ionian, Mixolydian and Lydian

Just like a major or minor scale, a MODE is a scale of eight notes in alphabetical order. A mode can begin on any scale degree of a major scale using the key signature of the parent scale.

In the key of C, for example, a mode can begin and end on C (I), on D (ii), on E (iii), etc.—no sharps or flats would be used. There are seven modes altogether and each has a Greek name. In the key of C, the modes are:

Beginning on   C — Ionian mode (major scale)
                D — Dorian mode
                E — Phrygian mode
                F — Lydian mode
                G — Mixolydian mode
                A — Aeolian mode (natural minor scale)
                B — Locrian mode

To easily learn how to build any mode on a keynote, it is helpful to relate the keynote to a major or natural minor scale with slight alterations.

The following three modes relate to the major scale. (H = half step.)

IONIAN MODE— a major scale.

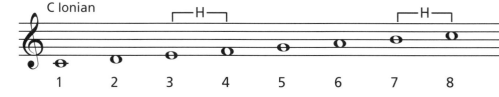

MIXOLYDIAN MODE— a major scale with the **7th lowered** a half step.

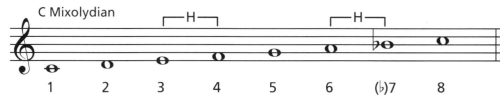

LYDIAN MODE— a major scale with the **4th raised** a half step.

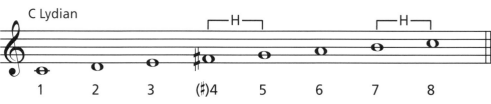

Exercises

1   Fill in the missing notes in the following Ionian modes.

G Ionian

a.

F Ionian

b.

2   Fill in the missing notes in the following Mixolydian modes.

G Mixolydian

a.

F Mixolydian

b.

3   Fill in the missing notes in the following Lydian modes.

G Lydian

a.

F Lydian

b.

Modes Related to the Minor Scale: Aeolian, Dorian, Phrygian and Locrian

The following four modes relate to the natural minor scale.

AEOLIAN MODE—
a natural minor scale.

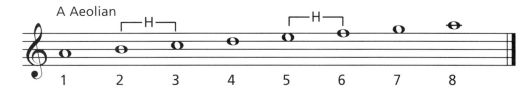

DORIAN MODE—
a natural minor scale with the **6th raised** a half step.

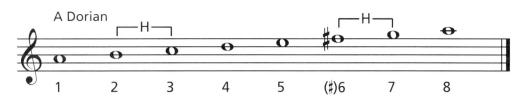

PHRYGIAN MODE—
a natural minor scale with the **2nd lowered** a half step.

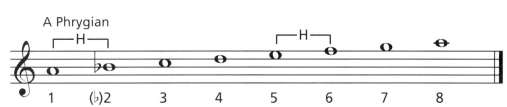

LOCRIAN MODE—
a natural minor scale with the **2nd** and **5th lowered** a half step. This mode was not used in ancient times and is only occasionally used in modern music.

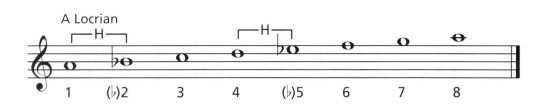

Exercises

1 Fill in the missing notes in the following aeolian modes.

E Aeolian

a.

D Aeolian

b.

2 Fill in the missing notes in the following dorian modes.

E Dorian

a.

D Dorian

b.

3 Fill in the missing notes in the following phrygian modes.

E Phrygian

a.

D Phrygian

b.

Examples:

1 Play Example 1, right.

2

i   iv   V7   i   V7   i

In Examples 3–6 you will play 2 scales each for letters a–e. The first scale will be major in Examples 3 and 4 and minor in Examples 5 and 6. If a scale contains a note in brackets [ ], first play the scale using the letter name indicated above the bracketed note and then play the scale a 2nd time using the actual note.

3 Play a major (or ionian) scale followed by a mixolydian scale (Example 3, right).

a.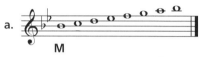
M

b.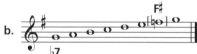
♭7

c.
♭7

d.
M

e.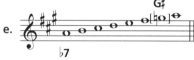
♭7

Page 100 from the Student Book:

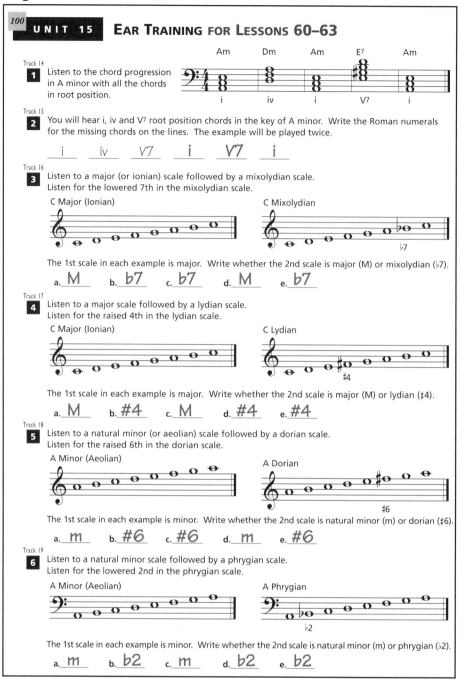

4 Play a major scale followed by a lydian scale (Example 4, above).

a.
M

b.

c.

d.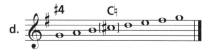

e.

5 Play a natural minor (or aeolian) scale followed by a dorian scale (Example 5, above).

a.
m

b.

c.

d.

e.

6 Play a natural minor scale followed by a phrygian scale (Example 6, above).

a.
m

b.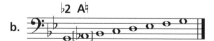

c.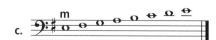

d.

e.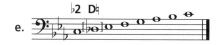

REVIEW OF LESSONS 60–63 · UNIT 15

1 Write the primary chords in the keys of B and G harmonic minor in root position.

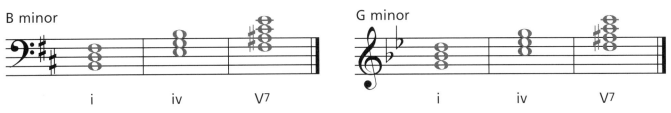

B minor   i   iv   V7

G minor   i   iv   V7

2 Write a D mixolydian mode.

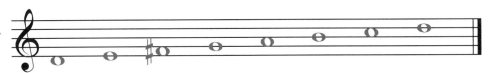

3 Write a B♭ lydian mode.

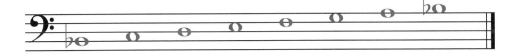

4 Write a B dorian mode.

5 Write a G phrygian mode.

6 Word Search: Solve the clues, then circle the words which may appear across, down, diagonally or backwards in the puzzle. Words may overlap.

a. Mode that is a natural minor scale.

b. Numbers to the right of chord symbols—I6 .

c. Three note chord consisting of a root, 3rd, 5th.

d. I IV I V7 I = a chord _____ .

e. Major triad with the 5th raised a half step.

f. Mode that is a major scale.

g. Three or more notes sounded together.

h. I, IV and V are the _____ triads in any key.

i. A G7 chord with the F in the bass = _____ inversion.

j. Mode that is a major scale with the 7th lowered a half step.

k. A _____ triad: root, minor 3rd, perfect 5th

l. Mode that is a natural minor scale with the 6th raised a half step.

m. Minor triad with the 5th lowered a half step.

n. Minor scale with the 7th raised a half step.

o. Mode that is a natural minor scale with the 2nd lowered a half step.

p. When the root of a chord is not the bottom note.

q. Mode that is a major scale with the 4th raised a half step.

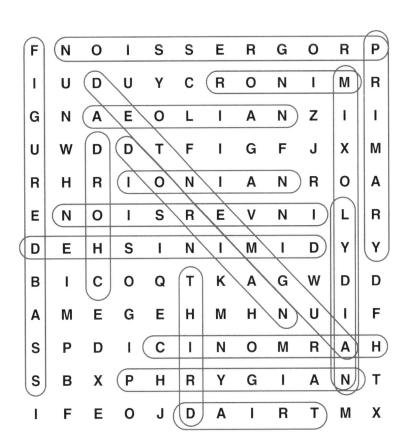

Harmonizing a Melody in a Major Key

To HARMONIZE a melody means to create a chord accompaniment for it. Since the I, IV and V (or V7) chords contain all the notes of the major scale, many melodies in a major key can be harmonized with just these three chords.

To determine the chords to be used, analyze the melody notes. Consult the following chart to see which chord is generally used with each melody note of a major scale. When more than one chord can be chosen, your ear should always be the final guide.

Scale Degree	Chord
1, 3, 5	I chord
2, 4, 5, 7	V (or V7) chord
1, 4, 6	IV chord

Here is a C major scale that is harmonized using only the I, IV and V (or V7) chords. When harmonizing with the V7 chord, the 5th is often omitted.

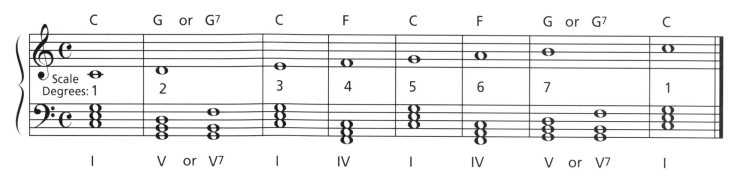

Most harmonizations usually begin and end with a I chord.
A V (or V7) chord usually precedes the last chord.

Exercises

1 Harmonize the G and F major scales with the I, IV, V (and V7) chords using inversions, where necessary, to achieve a smooth progression between chords (see page 87). Write the chord symbols above the staff and the Roman numerals below the staff for each chord.

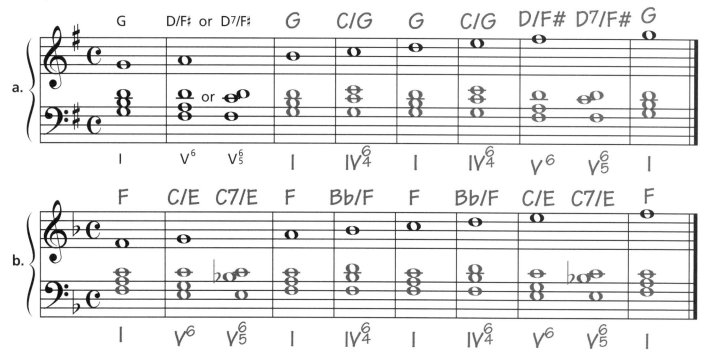

Broken Chords and Arpeggiated Accompaniments

BROKEN CHORDS

Another way to harmonize a melody is to break the chord notes so they are not played simultaneously.
When the notes of a chord are played together, it is called a BLOCK CHORD.
When they are not played together, it is called a BROKEN CHORD.

Block Chords 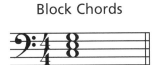 Broken Chords

ARPEGGIOS

When the notes of a chord are played sequentially, one after the other, it is called an ARPEGGIO. The word
arpeggio comes from the Italian *arpeggiare*, which means "to play upon a harp." An arpeggio may be extended
to an octave or more. Notice that the arpeggios below outline each note of the indicated chords in root
position. When a chord is repeated in the following measures, it is not necessary to repeat the chord symbol.

Schlaf in Guter Ruh

German Lullaby

Exercises

1 Add an arpeggiated accompaniment to the melody below. Use quarter notes on each beat based
on the indicated chords in root position.

It Rained A Mist

American Folk Song

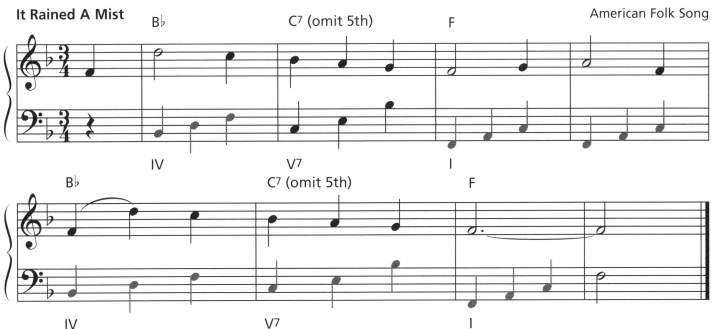

Passing and Neighboring Tones

Most melodies include tones that are not part of the chord used for the harmony. These non-chord tones are called NON-HARMONIC TONES. When a melody passes from one chord tone to a *different* chord tone with a non-harmonic tone (a half or whole step) between, the non-harmonic tone is called a PASSING TONE.

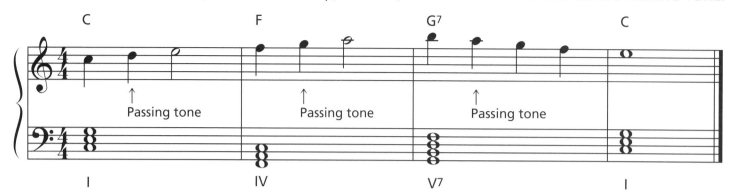

When a melody passes from one chord tone back to the *same* chord tone with a non-harmonic tone (a half or whole step) between, the non-harmonic tone is called a NEIGHBORING TONE. It is an UPPER NEIGHBORING TONE when it is *above* the chord tone, and a LOWER NEIGHBORING TONE when it is *below* the chord tone.

Passing and neighboring tones are non-harmonic and usually occur on a weak beat. These tones should not be a factor in your choice of a chord to harmonize a melody.

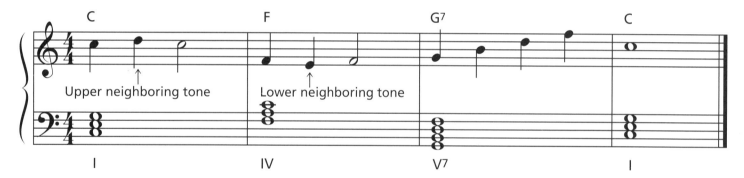

Exercises

1 Circle the upper neighboring tones and passing tones in the following melody. Identify each with U for the upper neighboring tones, or P for the passing tones.

London Bridge English Folk Song

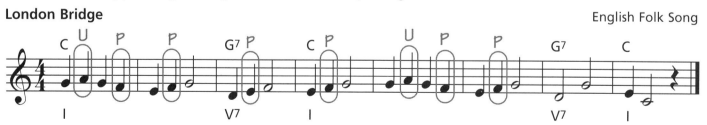

2 Circle the lower neighboring tones and passing tones in the following melody. Identify each with L for the lower neighboring tones, or P for the passing tones.

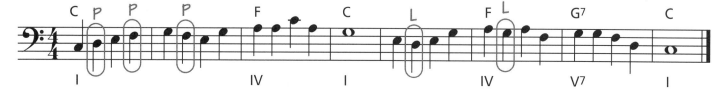

Composing a Melody in a Major Key

Just as you added harmony to a previously written melody, you can also COMPOSE (create or write) a melody to a previously written chord progression.

Begin by analyzing the chord progression and writing the Roman numerals under the chords—then add the chord symbols above the staff. By using chord tones and adding non-harmonic tones (passing and neighboring) to make the melody more interesting, you can compose your own unique melody.

Remember that the first and last note of a melody tends to be the root of the I chord, and a V (or V7) usually precedes the last chord. The numbers between the staffs refer to the melody notes. They are the intervals of the chords used in the bass accompaniment.*

Ghanaian Folk Song

*R=Root   3=3rd   5=5th   P=Passing Tone

Exercises

1 Analyze the harmony provided. Write the Roman numerals below the staff, then add the chord symbols above the staff. Write a melody (without rests) and circle any non-harmonic tones used.

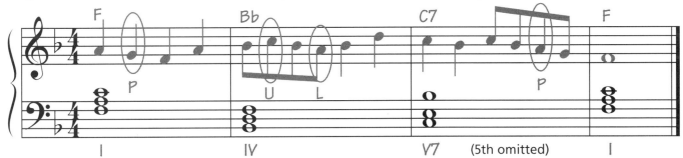

2 Analyze the harmony provided. Write the Roman numerals below the staff, then add the chord symbols above the staff. Write a melody (without rests) and circle any non-harmonic tones used.

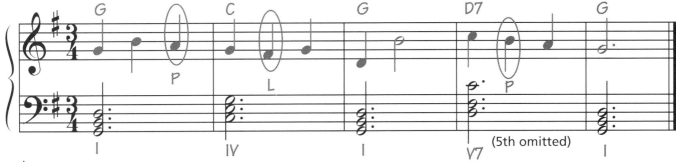

*Correct student answers may vary.

Track 20

1 Listen to the harmonization of a C major scale with a smooth chord progression.

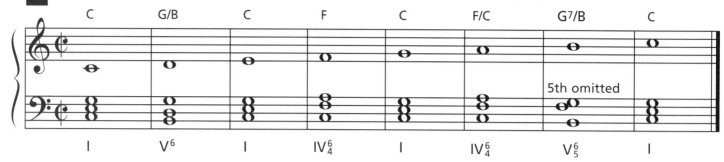

Track 21

2 Listen to the melody and chords. Write the missing chords in the bass clef, the Roman numerals (I or V$_5^6$) below the staff and the chord symbols above the staff. Omit the 5th in the V^7 chord. The example will be played twice.

Schubert Melody

Franz Schubert (1797–1828)

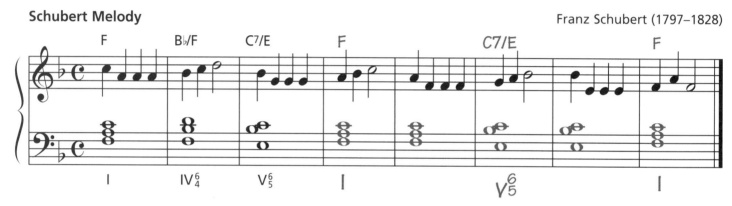

Track 22

3 Listen to the melody and chords. Circle the non-harmonic tones and write a P above the note if it is a passing tone, a U if it is an upper neighboring tone, and an L if it is a lower neighboring tone.

Shall We Gather At the River?

Robert Lowry (1826–1899)

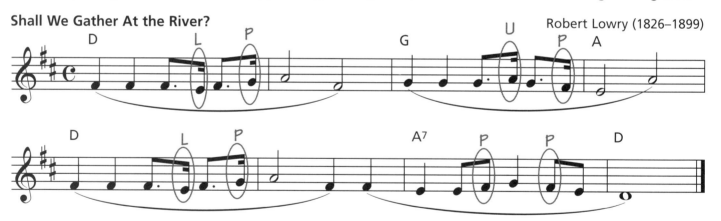

Track 23

4 Listen to the musical selection with an arpeggiated accompaniment.
Write the arpeggiated accompaniment in the bass clef. Omit the 5th in the V^7 chord.
The example will be played twice.

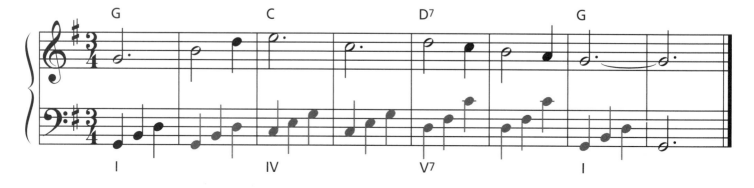

1 Fill in the blanks with the chord or chords that are generally used to harmonize a melody when a measure consists primarily of the following scale tones:

1, 3, 5 _____ I

2, 4, 5, 7 _____ V (or V7)

1, 4, 6 _____ IV

2 Harmonize the following melody with one chord in each measure except for measure 7 (there are chords on beats 1 and 4). Using I, IV and V7 chords only, write the chord symbol above the staff and the Roman numeral below the staff for each chord. Use a smooth chord progression—omit the 5th in the V7 chord.

Michael, Row the Boat Ashore

African-American Folk Song

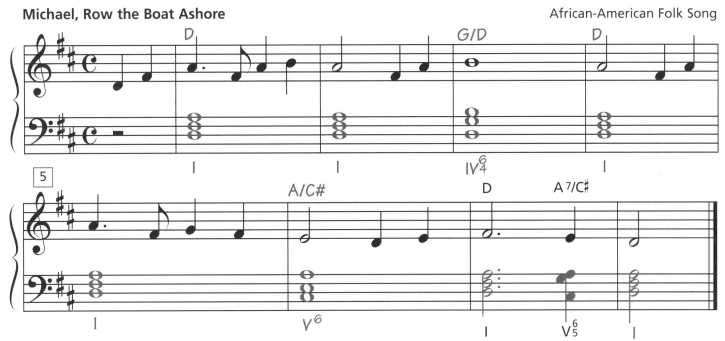

3 Most harmonies begin and end on a _____ I _____ chord, which is usually preceded by a _V (or V7)_ chord.

4 When a melody passes from one chord tone to a different chord tone with a non-harmonic tone (a half or whole step) between, the non-harmonic tone is called a _passing tone_.

5 When a melody tone returns to the same melody tone, the non-harmonic tone between is called a _neighboring tone_.

6 In the following melody, circle the non-harmonic tones and write a P above the note if it is a passing tone, a U if it is an upper neighboring tone, and an L if it is a lower neighboring tone.

Simple Gifts

Shaker Hymn

*7 Add an arpeggiated accompaniment to the melody. Omit the 5th in the V7 chord.

Dona Nobis Pacem

Anonymous

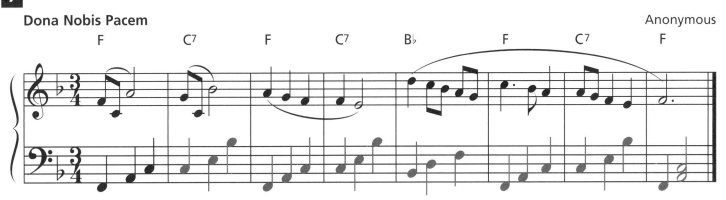

*Correct student answers may vary.

Harmonizing a Melody in a Minor Key

Harmonizing a melody in a minor key is similar to harmonizing a melody in a major key. Since the i, iv, and V (or V7) chords contain all the notes of the harmonic minor scale, many melodies in a minor key can be harmonized with just these three chords.

To determine the chords to be used, analyze the melody notes. Consult the following chart to see which chord is generally used with each melody note. When more than one chord can be chosen, your ear should always be the final guide.

Scale Degree	Chord
1, 3, 5	i chord
2, 4, 5, 7	V (or V7) chord
1, 4, 6	iv chord

Here is an A harmonic minor scale (raised 7th) that is harmonized using only the i, iv and V (or V7) chords.

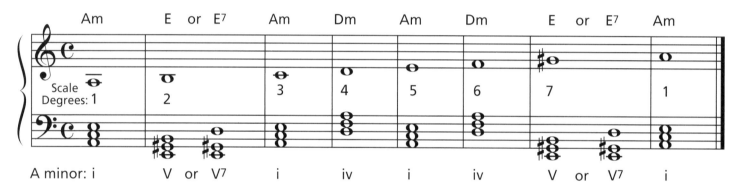

Most harmonizations usually begin and end with a i chord.
A V (or V7) chord usually precedes the last chord.

Exercises

1 Harmonize the E and D harmonic minor scales with the i, iv, V (and V7) chords using inversions, where necessary, to achieve a smooth progression between chords (see page 97). Write the chord symbols above the staff and the Roman numerals below the staff for each chord.

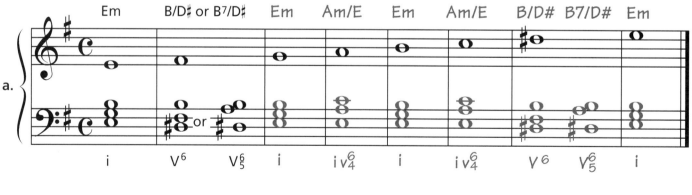

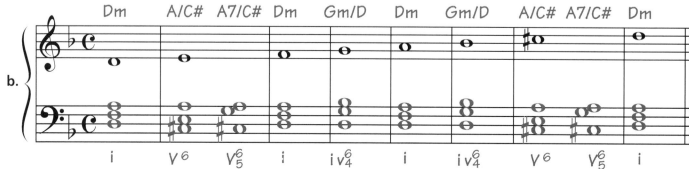

Composing a Melody in a Minor Key

Composing a melody in a minor key for an existing harmony is similar to composing a melody in a major key. The melody is created based on the tones in the chord accompaniment.

Begin by analyzing the chord progression and writing the Roman numerals under the chords—then add the chord symbols above the staff. By using chord tones and adding non-harmonic tones (passing and neighboring) to make the melody more interesting, you can compose your own unique melody.

Remember that the first and last note of a melody tends to be the root of the i chord, and a V (or V⁷) usually precedes the last chord. The numbers between the staffs refer to the melody notes. They are the intervals of the chords used in the bass accompaniment.*

Pat-A-Pan French Carol

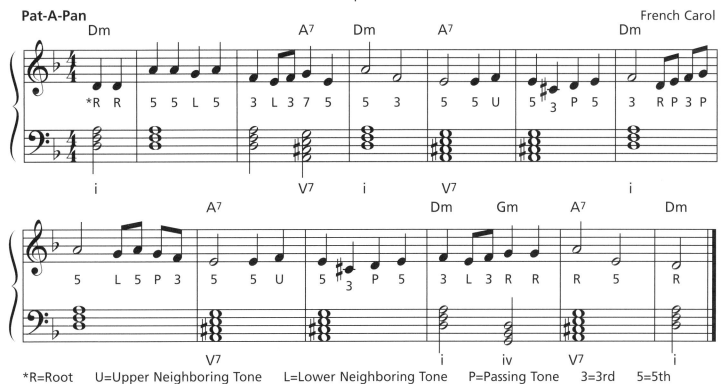

*R=Root U=Upper Neighboring Tone L=Lower Neighboring Tone P=Passing Tone 3=3rd 5=5th

Exercises

* **1** Analyze the harmony provided. Write the Roman numeral below the staff, then add the chord symbols above the staff. Write a melody (without rests) and circle any non-harmonic tones used.

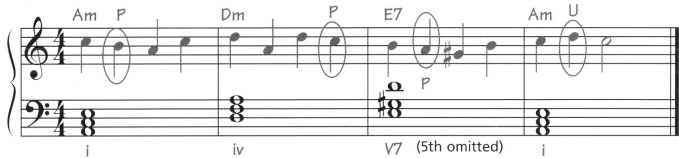

* **2** Analyze the harmony provided. Write the Roman numeral below the staff, then add the chord symbols above the staff. Write a melody (without rests) and circle any non-harmonic tones used.

*Correct student answers may vary.

12-Bar Blues Chord Progression

In addition to the major and minor chord progressions introduced on pages 87 and 97, another chord progression that is widely used is the BLUES progression. The music known as "the blues" has its roots in America's south where musicians combined west African rhythms and gospel singing with European harmonies. The blues can often be found in jazz, rock and pop music.

A BLUES CHORD PROGRESSION is usually 12 measures (or "bars") long, and while there are many variations, a traditional blues progression generally consists of the **I** chord (4 measures), the **IV** chord (2 measures), the **I** chord (2 measures), the **V** or **V⁷** chord (1 measure), the **IV** chord (1 measure), and the **I** chord (2 measures).

The C Major 12-Bar Blues Progression

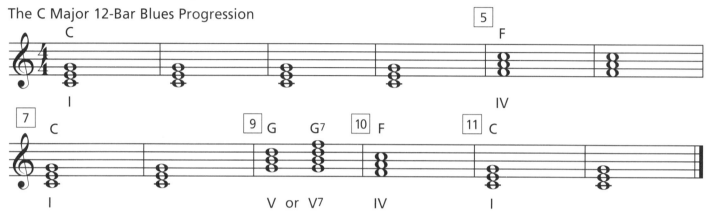

Exercises

1 Write the Roman numerals and the chord symbols for the chords in the following B♭ blues progression.

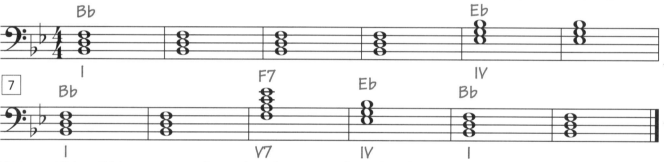

2 Write a 12-bar F blues progression using the I, IV and V⁷ chords.
Write Roman numerals below the staff and chord symbols above the staff.

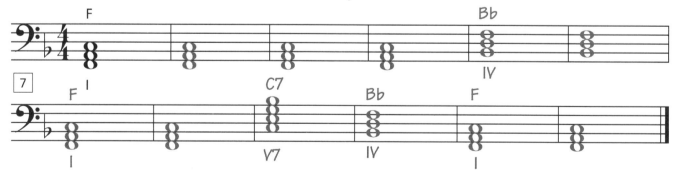

3 Write a 12-bar G blues progression using the I, IV and V⁷ chords. Write Roman numerals below the staff and chord symbols above the staff. Use a smooth chord progression and omit the 5th of the V7 chord.

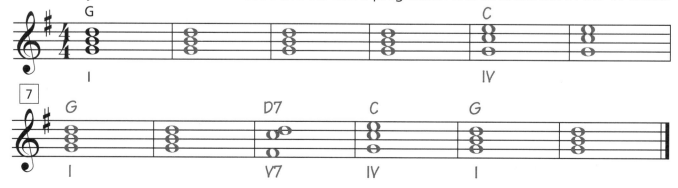

The Blues Scale

The special sound of the blues style is not only derived from the chord progression, but also from its unique scale. As compared to the major scale, the BLUES SCALE has only 7 notes and includes a flatted 3rd, 5th and 7th. The flatted notes are often called BLUE NOTES.

C Major Scale

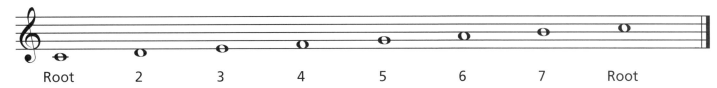

| Root | 2 | 3 | 4 | 5 | 6 | 7 | Root |

To change a major scale into a blues scale:
1. Remove the 2nd and 6th scale degrees
2. Flat the 3rd and 7th scale degrees
3. Add a flatted 5th

C Blues Scale

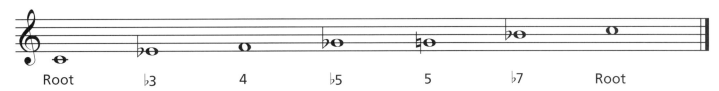

| Root | ♭3 | 4 | ♭5 | 5 | ♭7 | Root |

By writing or IMPROVISING (to spontaneously create a unique solo) the notes of a blues scale over a blues chord progression, the special sound of the blues is created.

Exercises

1 Fill in the missing notes in the following G blues scale.

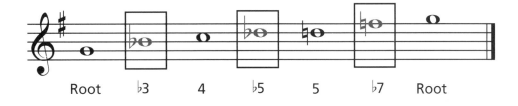

| Root | ♭3 | 4 | ♭5 | 5 | ♭7 | Root |

2 Write an F blues scale.

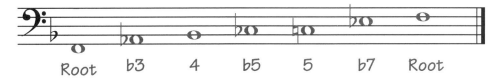

| Root | ♭3 | 4 | ♭5 | 5 | ♭7 | Root |

Page 112 of Student Book:

1   Play Example 1.

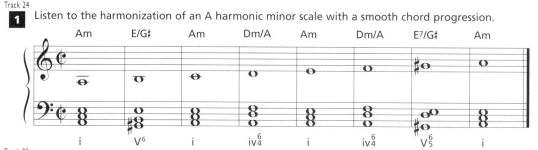

Track 24

1 Listen to the harmonization of an A harmonic minor scale with a smooth chord progression.

2   Play Example 2.

Track 25

2 Listen to the melody and chords. Write the missing chords in the bass clef (i or V$^6_5$ chords only), the Roman numerals below the staff and the chord symbols above the staff. Circle the non-harmonic tones and write a P above the note if it is a passing tone and an L if it is a lower neighboring tone. The example will be played twice.

3   Play Example 3.

Track 26

3 Listen to a 12-bar blues chord progression. A common practice in writing music is to use a / on each beat with the chord symbols written above. The rhythm section keeps time throughout the chord progression. The soloist can use the chord symbols as a guide to improvise.

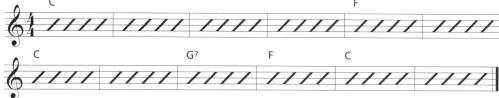

Track 27

4 Listen to a C major scale followed by a C blues scale.

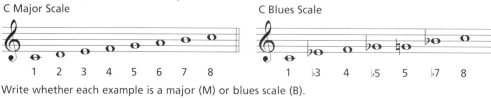

Write whether each example is a major (M) or blues scale (B).

a. M   b. B   c. M   d. B   e. B

4   Play a C major scale followed by a C blues scale (Exercise 4, above). The student writes whether each of the following is a major (M) or blues scale (B)

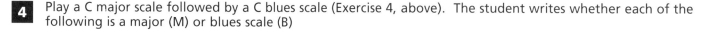

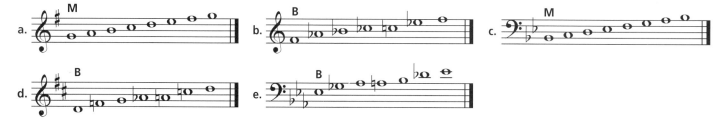

1 Which type of minor scale is usually used to harmonize melodies in a minor key? <u>harmonic minor</u>

2 Fill in the blanks with the chord or chords that are generally used to harmonize a minor melody when a measure consists primarily of the following scale tones:

1, 3, 5 <u>i</u> .   2, 4, 5, 7 <u>V (or V7)</u> .   1, 4, 6 <u>iv</u> .

3 Harmonize the following minor melody with one chord in each measure except for measure 3 (there are chords on beats 1 and 2). Using i, iv and V^7 chords only with inversions, write the chord symbols above the staff and the Roman numerals below the staff for each chord.

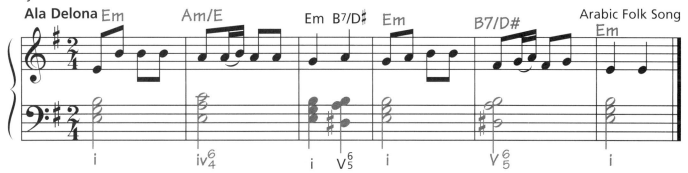

4 The 12-bar blues chord progression consists of the following chords (Roman numerals):

4 bars of <u>I</u> , 2 bars of <u>IV</u> , 2 bars of <u>I</u> , 1 bar of <u>V7</u> , 1 bar of <u>IV</u> , and 2 bars of <u>I</u> .

5 Write a 12-bar D blues progression. Write the chord symbols above the staff and the Roman numerals below the staff for each chord.

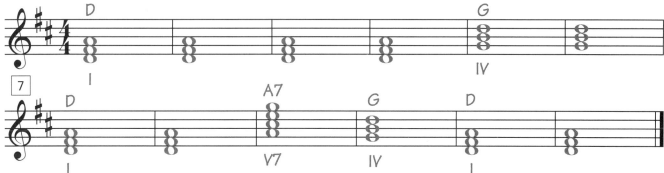

6 The blues scale has only <u>7</u> notes and includes a flatted <u>3rd</u> , <u>5th</u> and <u>7th</u> .

7 Write a G blues scale.

* 8 Write a 12-bar solo above the C blues progression. Use only notes in the C blues scale (C, E♭, F, G♭, G, B♭). Begin and end on C.

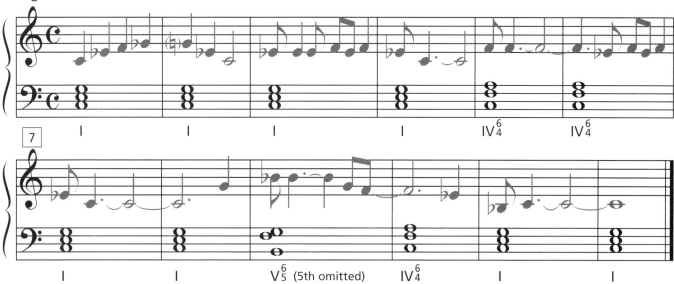

*Correct student answers may vary. When playing a blues scale in the right hand over a blues progression in the left hand, it is common to play the natural 3rd & 5th in the progression while playing the flatted 3rd & 5th in the solo above.

UNIT 18 LESSON 72

Basic Forms of Music—Motive and Phrase

Writing begins with the most basic unit—a letter of the alphabet. Letters are then combined into words, then sentences, paragraphs, chapters, and finally into larger works.

Similarly, music begins with a basic unit—the note. It is then combined into larger and larger melodic and/or rhythmic units, until a song or piece is created. Understanding the basic forms of music helps to understand how a composition is organized and structured.

A MOTIVE is a short melodic, rhythmic or harmonic element that is used repeatedly throughout a piece. Most music is based on the development and expansion of one or more motives. Perhaps the most well-known motive in classical music is the four note pattern used in the first movement of Beethoven's Symphony No. 5:

After its introduction, this melodic motive is used repeatedly in its original form, then later in transposition and other variations. The rhythmic pattern of this motive also appears as a motive in the 3rd and 4th movements.

A PHRASE is a short section of music that may be either a complete or incomplete musical idea. A phrase may contain one or more motives in their original form(s) or in some variation.

When one is speaking, the end of a phrase occurs when the speaker takes a breath, usually at a comma — there is a moment of pause. The end of a musical phrase provides a "lift" or breath for the instrumentalist or singer.

To demonstrate the way a phrase works, say the words of the following song, taking a breath (,) or pause at the end of each section.

Mary Had a Little Lamb   Traditional Folk Song

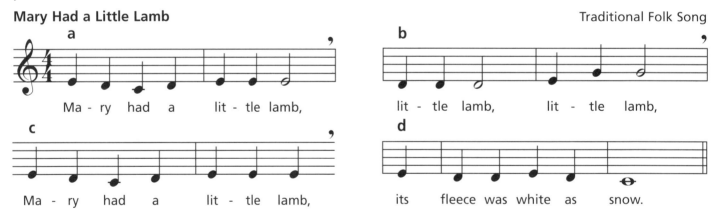

Each breath or pause was the end of a phrase. Now sing the rhyme and notice that the phrases of the music match those of the text.

Exercises

1 Which two phrases are similar in "Mary Had a Little Lamb?" #__1__, #__3__.

2 Circle the number of phrases in the following example: 1 ② 3 4

Baa, Baa Black Sheep   American Folk Song

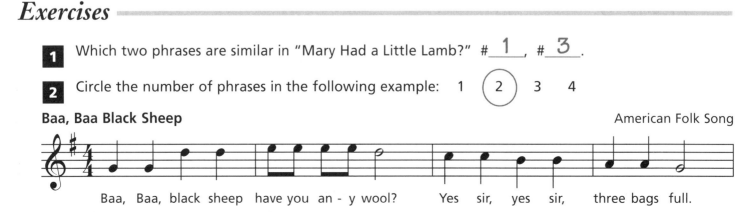

A B (Binary) Form

In music, several phrases can be combined to form a complete section (or part). In TWO-PART FORMS, called AB (or BINARY FORM), the musical material of the first (or A) section contrasts with the second (or B) section. Sometimes the two sections may share a motive or end similarly, but each section is musically distinct from the other.

Variety and contrast is achieved in each section through differences in many *elements* such as melody, rhythm, harmony, time signature and tempo. For instance, in "Go, Tell It On the Mountain," the first measure of the A section features an ascending melody with quarter notes, as compared with measure 1 of the B section which has a descending melody and a rhythm of a half note, dotted 8ths and 16th notes.

The melodic and rhythmic contrasts continue throughout each section. The time signature remains the same for the two sections and the harmony is similar, differing primarily in the final chord of each section.

"Go, Tell It On the Mountain" is an example of AB form.

Go, Tell It On the Mountain

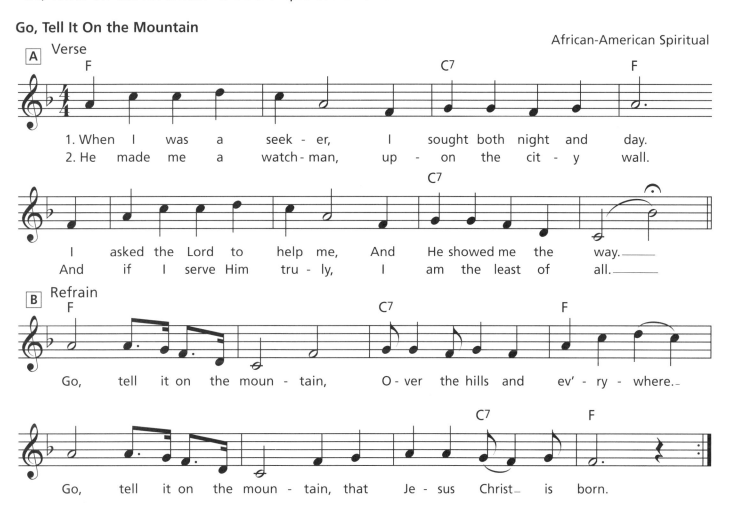

A VERSE is a section of a song that tells a story and changes with each repetition, which is followed by the REFRAIN (or CHORUS), a section of a song that is repeated after each verse. The song format of verse and refrain is typical of AB form.

Exercises

1 Circle the letter of the refrain section of "Go, Tell It On the Mountain."   A (B)

2 Circle the letter of the verse section of "Go, Tell It On the Mountain" that ends on a V⁷ chord. (A) B

3 Name two elements that make the music of the A section different from the B section:

____rhythm____   ____melody____ .

UNIT 18 **LESSON 74**

A B A (Ternary) Form

THREE-PART FORMS, called ABA (or TERNARY FORM), consist of two musically distinct sections as does AB form. In this form, however, there is **A**, a statement; **B**, a contrasting statement of new material; and **A**, a restatement of the A section. This is one of the most common forms found in all types of music, from folk songs to symphonies.

Swing Low, Sweet Chariot

African-American Spiritual

Exercises

1 Which section of "Swing Low, Sweet Chariot" is the verse? _____ B _____

2 Which section of "Swing Low, Sweet Chariot" is the refrain? _____ A _____

3 How many phrases are in: the A section? __4__ the B section? __4__

Rondo Form

A RONDO is a form that consists of an A section alternating with other contrasting sections of musical material. A is the recurring section. The most common types of rondo form are:

A B A B A — A B A C A — A B A C A B A.

"La Raspa" is an example of a rondo.

La Raspa

Mexican Folk Song

Exercises

1 What is the form of "La Raspa"? (Circle one) A B A B A (A B A C A) A B A C A B A

2 Which section prominently features eighth and quarter note rests in its motive? __A__

3 Which section differs harmonically from the others? __C__

UNIT 18 EAR TRAINING FOR LESSONS 72–75

Page 118 of the Student Book:

Examples:

1 Play Example 1, right.

2

Symphony No. 5 in C Minor, Op. 67

Ludwig van Beethoven (1770–1827)

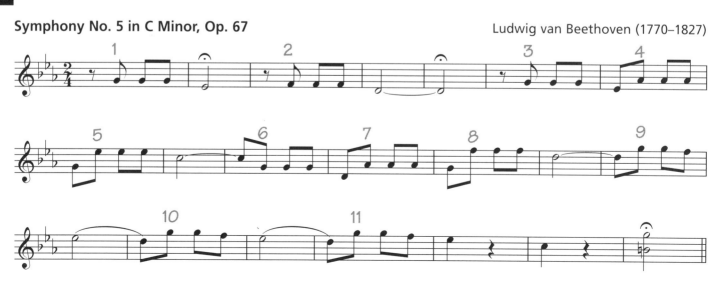

Twinkle, Twinkle, Little Star

French Folk Song

3

4 Play Example 4, *Scarborough Fair.*

Simple Gifts

American Shaker Tune

5

Get On Board

African-American Spiritual

6

Home on the Range

American Folk Song

7

8 Play Example 8, *Shoo, Fly.*

9

Für Elise

A

Ludwig van Beethoven

Poco moto

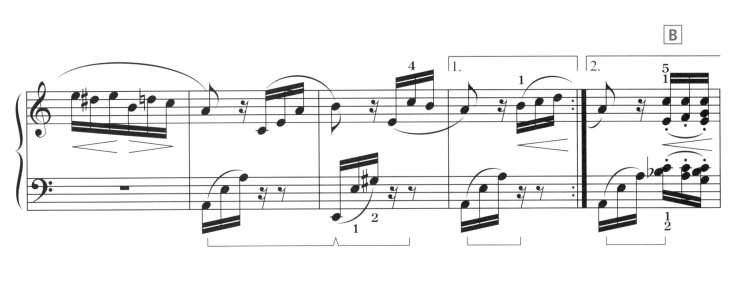

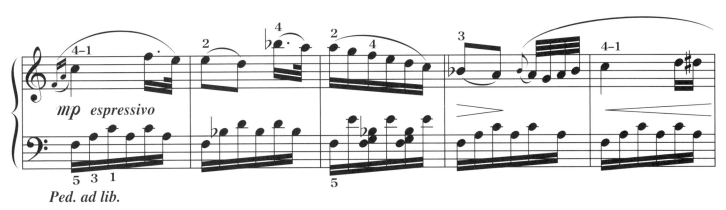

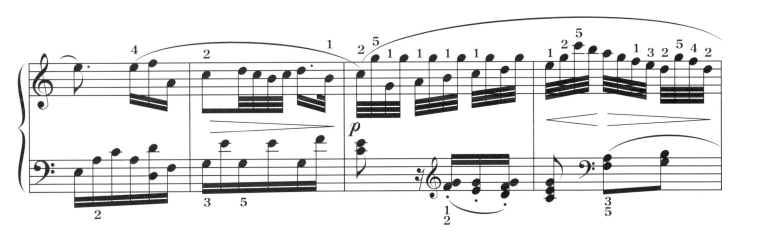

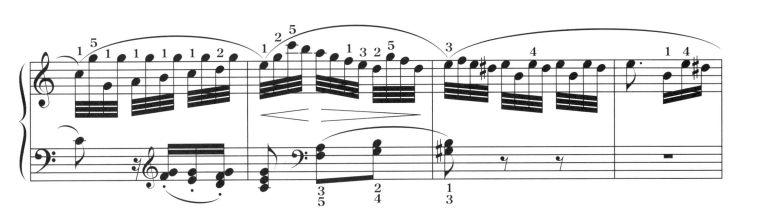

1 Mark the phrases, using curved lines over the entire phrase.

How many phrases are there? ___4___

Mistletoe Gifts   French Canadian Folk Song

Luck to the mas-ter and the mis-tress, Luck to the peo-ple dwell-ing here, Wheth-er a

cot - tage or a cast - le, Luck to you all and good New Year!

2 Two-part forms are also called ___A B___ or ___binary___.

3 What is the form of the following song? (Circle one)   AB   (ABA)

   a. Write the letters above the music at the starting point of each section.
   b. How many phrases are in the B section? ___4___

Trampin'   African-American Spiritual

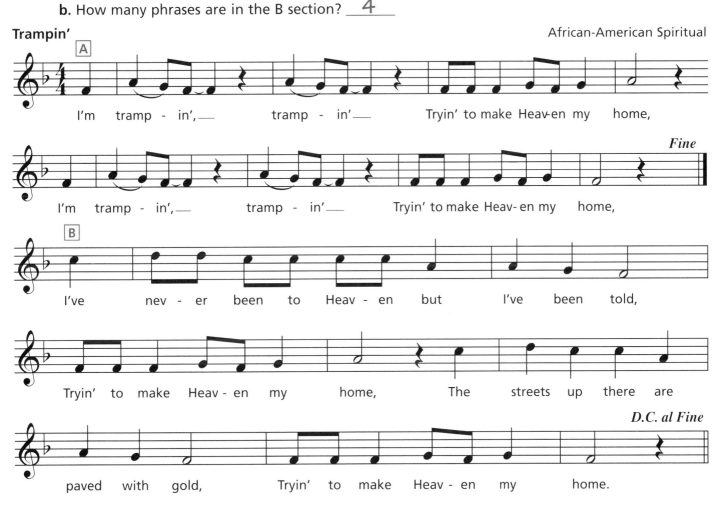

I'm tramp - in',— tramp - in'— Tryin' to make Heav-en my home,

I'm tramp - in',— tramp - in'— Tryin' to make Heav-en my home,

Fine

I've nev - er been to Heav - en but I've been told,

Tryin' to make Heav - en my home, The streets up there are

D.C. al Fine

paved with gold, Tryin' to make Heav - en my home.

4 The part of a song that tells a story is called the ___verse___.

5 Another name for the chorus section of a song is ___refrain___.

6 Three-part forms are also called ___ABA___ or ___ternary___.

7 The most common forms of a rondo are:
   a. ___ABABA___   b. ___ABACA___
   c. ___ABACABA___

GLOSSARY & INDEX OF TERMS & SYMBOLS
Includes all the terms and symbols used in Book 3 and the page on which they are first introduced.

AB (BINARY) FORM Two-part form where the musical material of the first (or A) section contrasts with the second (or B) section, i.e., verse and refrain song format (p. 115).

ABA (TERNARY) FORM A three-part form consisting of an A, a statement; B, a contrasting statement of new material; and A, a restatement of the A section (Ternary Form) (p. 116).

ACCOMPANY To play along with. A chord progression is used to accompany a melody (p. 87).

AEOLIAN MODE A natural minor scale, or A to A on the white keys of the piano (p. 99).

ARPEGGIO The notes of a chord played sequentially, one after the other (p. 103).

AUGMENTED TRIAD
A major triad that has been made larger by raising the 5th by ½ step (p. 93).

BAROQUE PERIOD The period of music from 1600–1750 (p. 86).

BINARY FORM AB or two-part form (p. 115).

BLOCK CHORD
The notes of a chord are played together (p. 103).

BLUE NOTES The flatted 3rd, 5th and 7th scale degrees of the blues scale (p. 111).

BLUES Music with roots in America's south where musicians combined west African rhythms and gospel singing with European harmonies (p. 110).

BLUES CHORD PROGRESSION
Usually 12 measures (or "bars") long, traditionally consisting of the I chord (4 measures), the IV chord (2 measures), the I chord (2 measures), the V or V7 chord (1 measure), the IV chord (1 measure), and the I chord (2 measures) (p. 110).

BLUES SCALE An altered major scale containing only 7 notes and including flatted 3rd, 5th and 7th scale degrees (p. 111).

BROKEN CHORD The notes of a chord played one at a time in any order (p. 103).

CHORD PROGRESSION When chords move from one to another, i.e., I IV V7 I (p. 87, 97).

CHORUS See Refrain (p. 115).

CLOSE POSITION Notes of a chord are spaced within an octave (p. 83).

COMPOSE To create or write a melody or chord progression (p. 105).

DIMINISHED TRIAD
A minor triad that has been made smaller by lowering the 5th by ½ step (p. 93).

DORIAN MODE A natural minor scale with the 6th raised a half step, or D to D on the white keys of the piano (p. 98).

FIGURED BASS
Numbers added to the Roman numeral of a chord to indicate the inversion of the chord to use (p. 86).

HARMONIC MINOR SCALE Raises the 7th tone of the natural minor scale by ½ step ascending and descending. Most frequently used type of minor scale (p. 91).

HARMONIZE To create a chord accompaniment for a melody (pp. 102, 108).

IMPROVISE To spontaneously create a unique solo (p. 111).

INVERSION The notes of a triad are rearranged and a tone other than the root is the bottom note of the chord (p. 83).

1st INVERSION
The notes of a triad are rearranged so the 3rd is the bottom note of the chord (p. 83).

2nd INVERSION
The notes of a triad are rearranged so the 5th is the bottom note of the chord (p. 84).

3rd INVERSION
The notes of a V7 chord are rearranged so the 7th is the bottom note of the chord (p. 85).

IONIAN MODE A major scale, or C to C on the white keys of the piano (p. 98).

LOCRIAN MODE A natural minor scale with the 2nd and 5th lowered a half step, or B to B on the white keys of the piano (p. 98).

LOWER NEIGHBORING TONE Non-harmonic tone a half or whole step below and between two of the same chord tones. It usually occurs on a weak beat (p. 104).

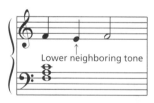
Lower neighboring tone

LYDIAN MODE A major scale with the 4th raised a half step, or F to F on the white keys of the piano (p. 98).

MELODIC MINOR SCALE Raises the 6th and 7th scale tones of a natural minor scale by ½ step when ascending. It descends the same as the natural minor scale (p. 91).

MINOR TRIAD Triad consisting of a root, minor 3rd & a perfect 5th. In major keys, triads with the root on the 2nd, 3rd or 6th scale degrees (p. 92). In minor keys using the harmonic minor scale, triads with the root on the 1st or 4th scale degrees (p. 96).

MIXOLYDIAN MODE A major scale with the 7th lowered a half step, or G to G on the white keys of the piano (p. 98).

MODE A system of scales that began in ancient Greece. It consists of eight notes in alphabetical order (p. 98).

MOTIVE A short melodic, rhythmic or harmonic element used repeatedly throughout a piece (p. 114).

NATURAL MINOR SCALE Scale using only the tones of the relative major scale and beginning on the 6th tone (p. 91).

NEIGHBORING TONE Non-harmonic tone a half or whole step above or below and between two of the same chord tones. It usually occurs on a weak beat (p. 104).

NON-HARMONIC TONES Non-chord notes or tones which are not part of the existing chord (p. 104).

OPEN POSITION Notes of a chord are spaced greater than an octave (p. 83).

PASSING TONE Non-harmonic tone melodically placed a half or whole step between one chord tone and a different chord tone, usually occurring on a weak beat (p. 104).

PHRASE A short section of music which may be either a complete or incomplete musical idea (p. 114).

PHRYGIAN MODE A natural minor scale with the 2nd lowered a half step, or E to E on the white keys of the piano (p. 98).

PRIMARY TRIADS I, IV and V chords in a major key. For a minor key, the harmonic minor scale is usually used to determine the i, iv or V chords (p. 96).

REFRAIN A section of a song that is repeated after each verse (chorus) (p. 115).

RELATIVE MAJOR SCALE Made up of notes beginning on the 3rd tone of the relative minor scale (p. 90).

RELATIVE MINOR KEY
Key signature that is the same as that of the relative major key (p. 90).

C Major/A Minor

RELATIVE MINOR SCALE Scale made up of notes beginning on the 6th tone of the relative major scale (p. 90).

RONDO FORM Contrasting sections of musical material followed by repeated A sections. Commonly A B A B A, A B A C A or A B A C A B A (p. 117).

TWO-PART FORM AB or BINARY FORM (p. 115).

TERNARY FORM ABA form (p. 116).

THREE- PART FORM ABA or Ternary form (p. 116).

UPPER NEIGHBORING TONE Non-harmonic tone a half or whole step above and between two of the same chord tones. It usually occurs on a weak beat (p. 104).

Upper neighboring tone

VERSE Section of a song that tells a story and changes with each repetition, followed by the refrain (p. 115).

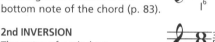

Grade Form for Ear Training and Review Pages

School Term _____   Class _____

Student Name	Book 1												Book 2					
	Unit 1		Unit 2		Unit 3		Unit 4		Unit 5		Unit 6		Unit 7		Unit 8		Unit 9	
	ET	R	ET	R	ET	R	ET	R	ET	R	ET	R	ET	R	ET	R	ET	R

Alfred's Essentials of Music Theory
Grade Form for Ear Training and Review Pages

School Term _____ Class _____

Student Name	Book 2 (continued)				Book 3												
	Unit 10		Unit 11		Unit 12		Unit 13		Unit 14		Unit 15		Unit 16		Unit 17		Unit 18
	ET	R	ET	R	ET	R	ET	R	ET	R	ET	R	ET	R	ET	R	ET	R